MW00988213

HAPPILY INTERMARRIED

HAPPILY INTERMARRIED

Authoritative Advice for a
Joyous Jewish-Christian Marriage

Rabbi Roy A. Rosenberg
Father Peter Meehan
Reverend John Wade Payne

COLLIER BOOKS
MACMILLAN PUBLISHING COMPANY
NEW YORK
COLLIER MACMILLAN PUBLISHERS
LONDON

Collier Books
Macmillan Publishing Company
866 Third Avenue, New York, N.Y. 10022
Collier Macmillan Canada, Inc.

Library of Congress Cataloging-in-Publication Data
Rosenberg, Roy A., 1930–
    Happily intermarried : authoritative advice for a joyous Jewish
-Christian marriage / Roy A. Rosenberg, Peter Meehan, John Wade
Payne.
        p.   cm.
    Reprint. Originally published: New York : Macmillan, c1988.
    Includes index.
    ISBN 0-02-036430-X
    1. Interfaith marriage—United States.   2. Children of interfaith
marriage—United States.   3. Family—United States—Religious life.
4. Jews—United States—Families—Religious life.   I. Meehan,
Peter. II. Payne, John Wade, 1932–   . III. Title.
HQ1031.R67   1989
306.8'43—dc19   88-39042   CIP

Macmillan books are available at special discounts for bulk purchases for
sales promotions, premiums, fund-raising, or educational use.
For details, contact:

Special Sales Director
Macmillan Publishing Company
866 Third Avenue
New York, N.Y. 10022

10   9   8   7   6   5   4   3   2   1

Printed in the United States of America

CONTENTS

Contents

PREFACE

As practically everyone knows, intermarriage between Jews and Christians is occurring in epidemic numbers. A number of books have been written about the subject, but this book, we think, is unique.

First, it is a book by a rabbi, a priest, and a minister. We, the authors, have attempted to provide you, the reader, with some background in the religious traditions and some insights that might be helpful in making a religious intermarriage a happy and fulfilling experience.

Second, there are no statistics in this book. We do not think that graphs and numbers contribute very much to an understanding of interfaith marriage. Suffice it to say that there are many such marriages, and their number will increase.

Third, we have included no "celebrities" or well-known personalities in our examples of interfaith marriage. All of the families from whom we have drawn illustrative materials are ordinary people who could very easily be your own friends or relatives.

The main source from which we have drawn is our own varied experience working with interreligious families. We hope that what we have learned might be of value to you, as it has been to us.

Roy A. Rosenberg
Peter Meehan
John Wade Payne

1

CAN TWO RELIGIONS COEXIST IN ONE HOME?

If you are one of the thousands of people living the length and breadth of the United States who contemplate the possibility of an interreligious marriage, you know that you ask yourself this question perhaps over and over again: Can two religions coexist in one home? Our answer to you is *yes*. We do not want you to think that you will have no problems to solve, but no marriage is without its problems. People who live together in a covenant of respect for each other, a relationship that is based on caring and sharing, can solve their problems, and that includes religious ones. If the purpose of religion is to keep people apart, then perhaps we would be better

1

off without it. The purpose of religion, however, is to bring people together in mutual respect and concern.

There are so many interreligious marriages today because people live together in the same neighborhood, go to school and college together, and work together in offices, laboratories, or factories. Jews and Christians today share many things in common—ideals and values, styles of living, educational background. For most of them there is not too much that distinguishes a "Jewish way of life" from a "Christian way of life." This was not always so, however. A look at where we have come from will help us understand why so many of us do not find it difficult to fall in love with each other.

There are still many lands across the face of the earth where those who subscribe to one religious philosophy look upon those who subscribe to any other religious philosophy as "dirty," "ignorant," or "wicked." Sometimes these animosities break out into outright warfare. The daily newspaper can keep us current with such happenings. Most people in the U.S., however, do not remember that attitudes in our own country were not so different as recently as fifty years ago. Not that we ever had to endure the massacre of one religious community by another within our own borders, but the attitudes of disdain were quite common. The law itself never mandated the unfair treatment of anyone because of his or her religion, but ask a Jew who grew up in New York around 1920, or a Catholic who grew up in Alabama at about the same time, and he or she will very likely tell you that things were not always so pleasant. Maybe she was turned down for a job because she did not attend the right church. Maybe he could not

2

buy or rent a home in a particular neighborhood because the people who lived there did not want "his kind." Maybe he was beaten up on the way to or from school because his books had the wrong kind of religious symbol on the cover. The U.S., while it welcomed immigrants to these shores, was not always kind to them once they had landed.

It was not only people who had been in America for several generations who looked down on the immigrants and the strange religious forms they brought with them. The immigrants themselves, by and large, looked upon other immigrants as "dirty," "ignorant," perhaps even "wicked." They had grown up with these prejudices in Europe. There was no ecumenical movement that brought Jews, Catholics, and Protestants together with an emphasis on their common heritage. In the Europe from which these immigrants came, most Christians were not too fond of Jews and most Catholics would rather not have too much to do with Protestants, and these feelings were reciprocated in kind. Marriage across religious lines was not unknown in Europe, but when it occurred, it meant that either the man or the woman was giving up his religious community and social position to join that of his spouse. The event was not one to celebrate; it was a matter of scandal and shame. These feelings were transplanted to America, and hundreds of thousands, perhaps millions, of Jews and Christians (and in the latter group, Catholics and Protestants) grew up during the first half of this century looking upon each other as the "enemy." When they fell in love with each other, as happened from time to time, they engendered the same sensations of shame and scandal as they would have in Europe. The very wealthy and the very poor could "get away" with marriage across religious lines—the wealthy because they had enough means not to be concerned about what other people said, and the very poor because they were low enough on the social scale that what other people said could not push them any lower. The vast majority, however, did not marry across religious lines. They cared about what other people said and, for the most part, had no desire to break the taboo. A sexual liaison across the line was perhaps acceptable, but marriage was another story. After all, "nice" people did not do such things.

What has happened to change the situation? Why are Jews and Christians marrying each other in epidemic numbers? The reason is that the prejudices the immigrants brought over from Europe have finally been discarded. No longer do most Christians and Jews regard the other as the "enemy," to be avoided as much as possible except in the arena of commerce. Beginning with the 1950s the vast numbers of Jews and Christians have been going to the same colleges and growing up in the same neighborhoods. Protestants, Catholics, and Jews all speak the same kind of English; they all enjoy the same foods (usually pizza and hamburgers); and they see that the things uniting them are vastly more numerous, and to many of them more important, than the things dividing them.

A generation or two ago the things that divided them were most important to the majority of Jews and Christians. Jewish Sunday School texts, in discussing the history and background of the American Jewish community, always devoted a good bit of attention to Rebecca Gratz, a cultivated and aristocratic Jewish

4

woman of Philadelphia during the eighteenth and nineteenth centuries. She was much sought after in marriage, but she had the misfortune to fall in love with a Christian gentleman. Did they marry? Of course not. Rebecca never wavered from her conviction that her Jewish identity was the most important thing in her life, and to her this identity would be compromised beyond repair if she were to marry a Christian. Did she ever find a Jewish husband? Of course not, because she never ceased to love the man to whom she had given her heart; in this age one did not marry, assuming one was a "nice" person, if one cherished a love for someone else, though one might never see or have contact with that person after the initial attraction. Rebecca lived to a ripe age as a single woman, never regretting the love that she cherished, though it was never physically fulfilled, and never regretting her decision not to marry, for this was the destiny her faith and her God had decreed for her. In the Sunday School texts she is praised as a heroine who has left behind a model and an example for others to follow.

Is the typical Jewish woman of today likely to follow Rebecca's example? It is hardly likely, for most people today do not think of their religious identity as the dominant aspect of their personality. Most Jews, like most contemporary Christians, are likely to describe religion as a "strictly personal" affair. From the standpoint of Jewish tradition, religion as a "strictly personal affair" is a contradiction in terms. The emphasis in Judaism is not on individual salvation but on the life of the family and the total community that is made up of families. The emphasis is not so much on belief or faith as on following a way of life sanctified by tradition, a tradition that links the generations of the past with the present. Today, though, Jewish men and women, like many Christians, regard their religion as only one of many elements making up the individual self. Except for some truly Orthodox Jews, it is rarely the dominant determinant of behavior. The typical Jewish woman of today, faced with the dilemma of Rebecca Gratz, would immediately begin to plan her wedding to her beloved, and if things turned out right, they would live happily ever after.

American Jews generally define their Judaism as an ethnic, rather than a "religious," identity. They are "proud" of being Jewish, though they obey few of the prescriptions of Jewish ritual law and have little interest in theology. An American Jew today, more often than not, thinks of himself as a Jew in the same way that an Italian-American regards himself as Italian. It is an identity one bears with pride; it links him or her to a certain language and literature (perhaps two of them, Yiddish and Hebrew). It ties one to a cuisine and history, and provides a feeling of fellowship with others of similar background. It does not require any "religious" activities or beliefs. Many say they are not "religious" but "cultural" Jews. The vast numbers of American Jews who define themselves in these terms have no more problem with marrying someone who is not Jewish than Italian-Americans have with marrying someone who is not Italian. They might on occasion lament that their spouse doesn't comprehend all the "in-group" jokes or allusions, or that she doesn't know how to cook all of Mama's favorite dishes, but there is certainly no compelling reason to hold them back from marriage and founding a family. The pursuit of personal happiness is what motivates Jews and Christians to marry each other.

An interreligious couple planning a marriage generally discusses religion much more earnestly than a one-faith couple. In many instances both bride and groom seek to confront what their religious tradition means to them on a much deeper level than either one ever did before. In relatively few cases is there a desire to "convert" the marriage partner to one's own religion. There is usually a genuine respect for the religion of the other party. Religion is accepted as part of ethnic identity, and ethnic identity is a part of one's being, like height or eye color, that cannot be changed. It is a part of the self that, as a totality, is "loved" by the other party in the union. "Judaism" is part of a Jew, even one who is not too religious, and "Catholicism" is part of most Italians and Irish, even those who rarely go to church. This is accepted by most interreligious couples who decide to marry.

The fact that most Jews define their Jewish identity in ethnic terms is nothing new. In fact, this is the way Jewish law and tradition define it. One is a Jew if one is born of a Jewish mother or has undergone a ceremony of "conversion" to Judaism. Traditionally speaking, ritual practices and theological convictions make one a "good" or "committed" Jew, but they are not necessary as a confirmation of Jewish identity.

Christianity, however, was from its origin defined as a faith commitment. In theory, if one ceased to believe that Christian theology was true, then one was no longer a Christian. This is no longer the case today, except for some evangelical and fundamentalist Christians. Most Christian groups today include people who have their doubts about the literal truth of the "Virgin Birth" or the "Resurrection" of Christ, but there has been no movement to expel these people from the Church. Some Christians who marry Jews are no more attached to these beliefs than their Jewish partners. Other Christians who marry Jews remain committed to these beliefs, but they do not think that either their Jewish partner or the children they will have must share these beliefs in order to be "saved." We live in an age when, at least in the Western world, the emphasis is on individuality, and fewer and fewer people are convinced that subscribing to particular religious beliefs is what will get them into heaven. Some evangelical and fundamentalist Christians, however, remain wedded to the old commitments. Such people should not marry Jews, and Jews should not marry them, unless one or the other is willing to give up his or her religious commitment.

The majority of people who marry across religious lines today are not concerned that their partner share their religious convictions. They feel that two people who love and respect each other can hold different religious beliefs; although active in different religious communities, they can still share so many things in common that the religious difference is of minor importance. We do not think it unusual for a Democrat and a Republican to marry each other and found a family, and many people do not think that a Jew and a Christian marrying each other is any different. In fact, the presence of two religions in one home is often considered "enriching," and the opportunity that children have to absorb the cultural influences from both traditions is sometimes looked upon as an advantage.

8

This may be the case, of course, but it does not always work out that way; parents in an interreligious family have to carefully work out the religious orientation with which they want their children to grow up.

In an interreligious family are there frequent arguments over religious beliefs and practices? Very rarely. Family dynamics seldom cut across the issues that theologians consider important, such as God's election of Israel or Christ's death and resurrection to save suffering humanity. We doubt that many husbands and wives debate these issues or the lesser ones, such as the historicity of the crossing of the Red Sea and the miracles of healing attributed to Jesus. Interreligious families argue about the same things other families argue about: the best way to discipline a child, who to invite to a dinner party, how much to spend on furnishing the house. There are no specifically "Jewish" or "Christian" answers to these questions, though ethnic and cultural differences not related to religion as such may sometimes become apparent in an interreligious family.

Richard grew up in a German Lutheran family in Missouri, Elaine in a Long Island, New York, Jewish environment. Elaine's family was upper middle class, and the home furnishings were always reflective of this background. Richard's family, on the other hand, was more frugal; they did not overspend on home decoration because they knew that economic conditions in farm country could change from year to year, and also they were convinced that too much "show" was not nice. It is understandable, then, that Richard and Elaine would not see eye to eye on how to furnish their home. They eventually compromised on what they spent and on the style of the items they purchased. Some of their friends thought they had to work through religious problems before they came to an agreement on their home furnishings, but this was not the case at all. Coming from two different backgrounds contributed to the problem they had to work through together, but religion had nothing to do with it. German Lutherans who had grown up on Long Island would very likely absorb the standards with which Elaine had grown up, and Jews growing up in Missouri farm country would very likely want to furnish their home in the style of Richard's family. Richard and Elaine's example illustrates differences in cultural background that have nothing to do with religion.

Anthony and Susan do not even think of themselves as intermarried, though he is Italian Catholic and she is Jewish. They are both convinced that the family backgrounds out of which they come are so similar it would be wrong to characterize their union as an intermarriage. Both Italians and Jews have a strong emphasis on family togetherness, both like to serve lots of food, and both like to laugh and sing as much as possible. (These are broad generalizations, of course, but many people, including large numbers of interreligious couples, subscribe to them.) There are many Italian-Jewish couples who, like Susan and Anthony, see only the similarities and not the differences in the pattern of family life in which they grew up, and as a consequence regard their difference in religion as insignificant when placed in the total context of their life.

Can two religions coexist in one home? This book will try to show you that indeed they can, that interreligious families can be found all over. Jews and Christians are marrying each other and having children who grow up to be happy and well adjusted. The prejudices of the past have been forgotten by many today, and people more and more are able to relate to one another as individuals, appreciating and respecting one another across religious, ethnic, and racial lines.

At Dawn's wedding reception, the bride overheard two of the older guests in the ladies' room: "She's such a lovely girl, it's too bad she's not Jewish." At the end of the evening she had occasion to return to the ladies' room, and this time she overheard: "He's such a fine boy, it's too bad he's not Catholic." Some in the older generation can accept interreligious marriage even though they have been trained to regard it as "too bad" that both bride and groom are not of the same religion. More and more in the younger generation, however, don't think that it is "too bad." What helped to make someone a "lovely girl" could be that she was raised as a Catholic, while what helped to make her husband a "fine boy" could be that he was raised as a Jew. The fact that they came together, many people now say, is not "too bad." It could very well be all to the good, both for themselves and for the society to which they belong.

2

WHAT A CHRISTIAN SHOULD KNOW ABOUT JUDAISM

The first thing a Christian should realize about Judaism is that it is the religion of a specific people, the Jews. It is not the creed of a group of people who have come together because they subscribe to a set of theological convictions. It is the creed of a group of people who believe they share a common descent, in a physical, biological sense, from Abraham, Isaac, and Jacob. The various Christian churches, on the other hand, originated as associations of people who subscribe to a set of shared beliefs. In theory, one "becomes" a Christian through acquiescence to those beliefs; no one is "born" a Christian. (This is not to say that there aren't many people who are only "nominal" Christians, who are baptized as infants and go through life celebrating Christmas and Easter, but with little or no fully realized system of belief.)

In Judaism, one is definitely "born" a Jew; one does not have to share any of the beliefs of Judaism to be a Jew. It is like being Chinese or French or Eskimo; it is an ethnic identity that you can't get rid of, unlike membership in a Christian church.

Of course, in addition to those who are born into it, many people "convert" to Judaism. Conversion to Judaism is analogous to being adopted into a family. The convert, at the moment of his or her public acceptance of Judaism, is reborn as a child of Abraham and Sarah. In Christianity Abraham is the spiritual father of all believers. In Judaism he is revered as the biological father of all of his descendants, whether by birth or adoption. Scholars date Abraham about 1750 B.C.

If the Jews constitute a specific ethnic group, how come they are found all over the world? And even more to the point, how come there are Jews of every race and skin color? The reason is that during the time of the Roman Empire some Jews were exiled from their land and others left voluntarily, seeking greater opportunity in the cities of the world. Wherever Jews went, they intermarried with the inhabitants of the lands where they dwelled. Most of these marriages involved a conversion to Judaism since the laws of the religion prohibited a marriage to one who did not accept the religion. This is the reason Jews look like the people among whom they live: In Bombay, many are dark-skinned Indians; in Ethiopia, they are indistinguishable from their black Christian and Moslem neighbors; in Europe they look like Italians in Italy, like the English in London, and like the Slavic peoples in the lands of Eastern Europe. And in America they resemble the people of the many lands who have come to this, the melting pot of the nations of the world.

Of course, over the centuries there were not only conversions to Judaism but those who left Judaism too. In practically every country in Europe, the Middle East, and North Africa there are large numbers of people of part-Jewish ancestry, even though they may have been Christian or Moslem for generations. There are communities in Spain and Portugal where most of the people are of Jewish descent, even though they know nothing of Judaism.

The Jews who moved out into the world gravitated toward the cities. Very few of them sought work as peasants, tilling the soil, although that had been the lot of their ancestors in biblical times. It was this attachment to the cities that impelled many Jews to cultivate intellectual pursuits. Their religion was also a spur to intellectual activity since it was the obligation of all Jewish men to be able to read and interpret Scripture and even the commentaries of the rabbis. It was this background that enabled many Jews, after they were granted rights of citizenship during the nineteenth century, to pursue careers in law, medicine, and the sciences. (While Jews have been in the forefront of intellectual and cultural pursuits in both Western Europe and America, it would nonetheless be wrong to think of all Jews as being particularly smart.)

Another factor that motivated many Jews toward intellectual achievement was religious persecution and anti-Jewish discrimination. A Jew had to work twice as hard to get ahead in his work or profession, so the saying went, in order for him to overcome the barriers erected against him. During the Middle Ages anti-Jewish laws were quite common throughout Europe. Jews often were restricted to a certain quarter in a city, the "ghetto." They sometimes were prohibited from certain kinds of work and had to wear distinctive clothing that would subject them to ridicule. They were taxed heavily and sometimes were herded into the local synagogue to hear a sermon from a representative of the Church extolling the truths of Christianity as opposed to the "errors" of Judaism. The long heritage of anti-Jewish teaching and legislation culminated in the Holocaust, the attempt during World War II to exterminate all the Jews of Europe.

The answer of the Jewish people to the heritage of anti-Jewish persecution was the State of Israel. A Jewish homeland on the ancestral soil, so the hope went, would enable the people to develop its full potential, free of the oppression of foreigners. Israel exerts a powerful spiritual pull on many Jews throughout the world, and few are the Jews who are unconcerned for its welfare.

THE JEWISH FAITH AND PEOPLE—A VERY SHORT HISTORY

The religion known as Judaism begins with the premise that the God of Abraham, Isaac, and Jacob established a covenant with them that was to be transmitted to their descendants: He would be their God, and they would be His people. Jacob, who was also known as

Israel ("he who strives with God"), was the father of twelve sons, the ancestors of the twelve tribes of Israel. Ten of the twelve tribes disappeared from the historical scene after being conquered by Assyria around 700 B.C. Only the tribe of Judah, along with the associated tribe of Benjamin and the priestly clan of Levi, has retained its identity over some three thousand years to the present day. "Jew" is a shortened form of "Judean"; the religion of the Judeans was Judaism.

According to the Bible, Jacob and his household settled in Egypt after escaping from a famine that afflicted their homeland of Canaan (known later as Israel or Palestine). The Egyptians enslaved the Israelites, however, and they cried out to the God of their ancestors for deliverance. This God appeared to Moses, of the priestly family of Levi, who then defied the pharaoh of Egypt and led his people from bondage into freedom, guided by the hand of God amidst many "signs and wonders." This is the great redemptive act of God that gave birth to the nation of Israel. It is commemorated every year at Passover when every Jew is bidden to regard himself as having been enslaved in Egypt and then liberated from bondage through the mighty acts of God. It is Moses who brought the unique name of God to the Israelites: *Yahweh,* which means either "He who is" or "He who causes to be." Judaism considers this name too sacred to pronounce. The usual substitution for it is *Adonai* ("the Lord").

Moses is revered not only as the liberator but also as the lawgiver and teacher (rabbi) of Israel. Judaism elaborates upon God's revelation at Mount Sinai, when the Ten Commandments were heard not only by those then alive but also by all the generations yet unborn.

This revelation constituted a covenant that was made with all Jews for all time. It is embodied in the Torah, the "teaching" that God is supposed to have given by the hand of Moses. In a narrow sense the Torah is the Pentateuch, the "five books of Moses." In a wider sense it is the entire Hebrew Scriptures (Old Testament), including Pentateuch, Prophets, and Writings. In its widest sense the Torah is all of Jewish teaching from the earliest times to the present day. The early rabbis summarized all of the law of the Torah in one verse: "You shall love your neighbor as yourself; I am the Lord" (Leviticus 19:18).

After the death of Moses, the Israelite tribes conquered their ancestral homeland of Canaan. Around 1000 B.C. David unified the tribes and established a royal dynasty in Jerusalem. There, too, the Temple of Yahweh was built, regarded as the earthly residence of the deity. Worship at the Temple, conducted by the Levitical priests, revolved primarily about animal sacrifice. Prophets also flourished in Israel, many of them not merely soothsayers who predicted the future but moral teachers who emphasized the primacy of ethics over ritual. The dynasty of David and the Temple were destroyed by Babylonian conquerors in 586 B.C., with many Jews exiled to Babylon. When Persia conquered Babylon some years later, the Jews were given the opportunity of returning to Jerusalem and reconstituting their community there. Some did, but many preferred to remain in Babylon. Thus the "dispersion" or "diaspora" of the Jews began, with communities of Jews outside of Palestine preserving their own religious traditions and looking to Jerusalem as their spiritual center.

About 330 B.C. Alexander the Great conquered the Persian Empire, and the Jews came under the influence of Greek culture and philosophy. Ever since then, Judaism has developed as a combination of ancient Near Eastern thought and Greek philosophical insights. Christianity, too, is the result of the combination of these two cultural traditions. The Jewish kingdom regained its independence for a short while in 165 B.C. when a successful revolt by those seeking religious freedom was led by the Maccabee family. The festival of Hanukkah commemorates this victory. It was not long, however, before Judea became part of the Roman Empire, as did all of the lands circling the Mediterranean.

One of the mistakes made by Christians and even a few Jews is in thinking that Judaism ceased its development with the close of the biblical period. If this were so, Judaism would still be offering animal sacrifices, but this mode of worship ceased with the destruction of the Temple in Jerusalem in A.D. 70.

A number of sects grew up in Judea during the Roman period. The most prominent was the Pharisees, who developed the concept of the "oral Torah" that accompanied and interpreted the written Scriptures. The oral Torah was the product of the rabbinic teachers who attempted to update or modernize the laws of the Pentateuch. To give an example, the Bible provides that all debts are to be canceled every seven years. Such a law was desirable in a simple agricultural society, but in a society based on Greek-style urban communities it became impossible to live with. No one would lend money to the poor, for they knew it would not be paid back. The rabbis provided, therefore, that the debt should be placed in the hands of the court, collectible even if the seventh year intervened. In this way the poor were safeguarded, and loans continued to be made to them. The oral Torah eventually became so vast that it had to be written down. It took the form of the Talmud, which contains the enactments and discussions of the rabbinic teachers of both Palestine and Babylonia from the pre-Christian centuries to A.D. 500. The Talmud includes not only law but also ethical and historical material, and even an occasional joke. It, along with the Hebrew Bible, is the basic sacred text of Judaism and is the major object of study in traditional rabbinic academies to this day.

During the Roman occupation of Palestine, the yearning for a Messiah spread among many Jews. The word "messiah" means "anointed" and can refer to a king, priest, or prophet. The Essene sect, a monastic group governed by rigid rules, left behind a collection of writings that were discovered only recently: the Dead Sea Scrolls. These scrolls reveal that this sect awaited the coming of two "messiahs," one from the house of David and the other of priestly descent. The majority of Jews, however, were influenced by the tradition of the Pharisees, who looked toward the advent of a messianic king of the line of David, one who would inaugurate a kingdom of righteousness under God in place of the Roman government and the corrupt priesthood of the Jerusalem Temple. Messianic hopes were behind the revolt that caused the Romans to destroy Jerusalem in the year 70 and exile many Jews throughout the empire. Large Jewish communities had existed for centuries in Babylonia and in Alexandria (Egypt), but now Jews spread over many parts of Europe, into North Africa, southward to Yemen and Ethiopia, and even as far as India and China. For this reason Jews are to be found among all the major racial groups and skin colors on the face of the earth. Wherever Jews moved, though, they preserved the teachings of the Bible and Talmud, and the tradition of common descent from Abraham. They looked forward, too, to the redemption that would come in the future, modeled on the redemption of their ancestors who had been slaves in Egypt, for they were convinced that God does not forsake His people.

Besides the hope for earthly redemption in the days of the Messiah, Pharisaic Judaism also taught a belief in the resurrection of the dead. At the "end of days" souls would be restored to the bodies of the dead, and they would be raised for judgment, the wicked to be destroyed and the righteous to live for eternity. The early Christians also shared this belief. Accompanying the concept of bodily resurrection was a belief in the soul's sojourn in heaven after death. More precisely, it was the souls of the righteous who dwelt there in the presence of God. The souls of the wicked went to punishment.

Judaism was able to survive and thrive after the destruction of the Temple because the institution known as the synagogue had come into existence perhaps two centuries before that event. A synagogue (Greek for "community house") was a place where people gathered mornings and evenings for prayer, and a reading from the Pentateuch and the Prophets on Sabbaths and other sacred days. After the Temple was no more, the "service of the heart," which was prayer, replaced animal sacrifice as the sign of religious devotion. Prayer in a congregation was desirable, but it was not required; it could be offered by an individual wherever he or she might be. At the heart of the worship service every morning and evening was, and still is, this declaration: "Hear, O Israel, the Lord is our God, the Lord is One. You shall love the Lord your God with all your heart, with all your soul, and with all your might" (Deuteronomy 6:4). These are the same words that appear in the *mezuzah,* the inscribed parchment encased in a decorative container that is supposed to be affixed to the doorpost of every room in a Jewish household, or at least at the entrance to the house.

Synagogues may be grandiose cathedral-like structures, or they may function in the living room of a simple family home. They need not conform to any set architecture or style of decor. There are a few features, however, that are common to practically all synagogues. The Holy Ark, in which the scrolls of the Torah are kept, is usually set in the eastern wall, in the direction of Jerusalem. Above the Ark is the Eternal Light, either a flame or an electric fixture that is always kept lit. On either side of the Ark there is often a seven-branched candelabrum, derived from the golden candelabrum that was kept perpetually lit in the Temple of Jerusalem. In Orthodox synagogues the prayer leader, who may be a rabbi or a layman, always faces the Ark, not the congregation. In non-Orthodox synagogues the prayer leader usually faces the congregation.

Visitors who are not Jewish are always welcome at synagogue services. In Orthodox synagogues the service is mostly in Hebrew, so a visitor would likely wish to go with a friend who could explain what was being said. Conservative and Reform services are a mixture of Hebrew and English, and visitors who do not know

Hebrew ordinarily will have no trouble in following what is going on. Men and women sit together in non-Orthodox synagogues, but in Orthodox ones they are separated. Men at Orthodox and Conservative synagogues, even non-Jewish visitors, are expected to wear a *yarmulke* (skullcap) or other head covering as a mark of respect. This is not required in Reform Judaism. At all synagogues visitors should follow the example of the congregation in standing when others stand and sitting when they sit.

LAWS OF SEPARATION

The system of Jewish law originating in the Bible, and developed further in the Talmud and by later interpreters, is called Halacha (way). It includes civil and criminal law and ethical ideals, as well as more strictly "religious" matters such as holiday and liturgical practices. Part of the body of Halacha includes regulations whose primary purpose is to keep Jews separate from others so that the purity of tradition might be preserved. Foremost among these regulations are the dietary restrictions. The Bible prohibits the consumption of animals that do not both chew the cud and possess a split hoof. The pig is the chief example of such a prohibited animal. The Bible also prohibits the consumption of shellfish, since they lack fins and scales. In addition, other animals that are acceptable for Jews to eat must be slaughtered in the ritually correct way.

The Talmud took one of the Bible's laws, "You shall not cook the young in its mother's milk," and expanded it to prohibit the consumption of any meat at the same meal at which a dairy product is eaten. The rabbinic legislators went even further and decreed that separate dishes must be used for meat products and dairy products. Dishes or utensils that have been used for prohibited animals, or acceptable animals that have not been slaughtered in the correct manner, are also prohibited for Jewish use. Both the food and the utensils used by Jews must be *kosher* (fit).

The dietary regulations have the effect of restricting social relationships between the Jews who observe them and both those Jews who do not observe them and the entire non-Jewish world. In like manner, the laws prohibiting the marriage of a Jew to a non-Jew serve to restrict these relationships for the purpose of preserving the tradition from contamination. The Torah prohibited only the marriage of a Jew to a Canaanite. It was in the fifth century B.C., after the return from Babylon, that the authorities prohibited the marriage of a Jew to any non-Jew unless there was a conversion to Judaism. The marriage of a Jewish woman to a non-Jewish man is not acceptable, but nonetheless the children of the woman are considered Jewish. The tradition is far more disturbed by the marriage of a Jewish man to a non-Jewish woman, for in this case the children are not considered Jewish, and the man, by his action, has severed his family line from its descent from Abraham. Such children, though, upon their own volition, can seek conversion to Judaism.

A JEWISH VIEW OF JESUS

Many Jews and Christians, if asked to define the difference between Judaism and Christianity, say that Christians "believe in" Jesus while Jews don't. This is a very simple answer and, while it is not necessarily wrong, it doesn't explain much. From the Jewish point of view, Jesus was a human being, born to a Jewish father and mother, who was a teacher of religion and ethics during the first century. Christianity came to regard him not only as fully human but also as divine, which Judaism does not do. Jesus was called "son of God" by some Jews because this was a term applied to teachers and healers who were looked upon as filled with the "spirit of God." Later, the term "son of God" gave rise to the traditions about the miraculous birth of Jesus that are celebrated each year at Christmas. Jesus during his lifetime was hailed as "lord" by his followers, for they regarded him as their supreme master and teacher whose ethical instruction would make it possible for them to enter the impending kingdom of God. This term "lord" later helped Christians to look upon Jesus as divine since Jews spoke of God as "Lord" in order to avoid pronouncing the divine name Yahweh.

Jesus took it upon himself to bring the message of the kingdom of God to the poor. In that sense he was a revolutionary, though he did not advocate taking up arms against the government. He seems to have been heavily influenced by some of the Essene traditions. He denounced the ruling circles because of their disdain for the poor, in the way of the prophets of the Hebrew Scriptures. Feared as one who could incite the masses to rebellion, he was put to death. His followers thereaf-

ter looked upon him as the awaited Messiah, though
we have no evidence that Jesus ever publicly proclaimed
himself the Messiah during his lifetime. Instead, he
may have regarded himself as the expected prophet
who was to proclaim the coming of the kingdom of
God.

Jews do not look upon Jesus as divine. They do
respect him as a great religious teacher. The kingdom
of God surely could be said to be present if all people
lived by the ethical teachings of Jesus. What is difficult
for Jews to accept, however, is the teaching of the early
Church that, with the coming of Jesus, the Torah was
no longer in force, that Jesus had replaced the Torah
with himself. At first the Church taught that pagans
who wished to become Christians were exempt from
the laws of the Torah. Jews would have no problem
with this point of view. It was later that the Church
came to abrogate the laws of the Torah—circumcision,
Sabbath, dietary laws—with regard to Jews as well.
Jews could not accept this since the Torah was the
embodiment of the covenant, the link between Israel
and God that had been brought down from heaven by
the patriarchs and Moses.

THE HOLY DAYS OF JUDAISM

Many Jews, if asked to name the most important holy
day in Judaism, would give the wrong answer. The
correct answer is the Sabbath, which comes every week,
beginning Friday at sundown and extending until Saturday at sundown. Many Jews, if asked to describe how
the Sabbath should be observed, would again give the

wrong answer. While the Sabbath is a time for abstention from labor, it is also the most joyous day of the week. It is not a day for gloom and solitude, it is a day of eating, song, and dance. Since prayer and the study of the Scriptures are the most joyous activities for a traditional Jew, it is fitting that there be time for these pursuits on the most joyous day of the week. Sex, too, is not forgotten. The sexual union of husband and wife is especially commended on the Sabbath.

The Sabbath is the only festival mentioned in the Ten Commandments, both as a memorial of the creation of the world and as an opportunity to give rest to one's servants. Jews are bidden never to forget that they were themselves slaves, and they should always be conscious of the needs of those who labor. Like most of the other Jewish holidays, the day begins at sundown with the blessing of the light offered by the wife, for the woman is the light of the home. This is followed by the blessing of the wine, the symbol of joy, by the husband. The blessing of the bread is next, and then the festive meal. After the synagogue service in the morning, another festive meal is taken. At sundown on Saturday, as the Sabbath comes to its end, traditional Jews celebrate with song yet again in a gathering called "the escort of the Queen," for the Sabbath is personified as a bride, a queen, who comes to her people once a week bringing joy and blessing.

Of the holidays that come once a year, the day of the New Year (Rosh Hashana) is the first, followed ten days later by the Day of Atonement (Yom Kippur). These days are observed in September or October, about the time of the fall equinox. Though these days are penitential in nature, it is wrong to think of them as sad. They are, in fact, joyous occasions, for the assurance of God's pardon makes for happiness. Rosh Hashana begins with a festive meal at home as the holy day begins at sundown. Yom Kippur is preceded by a meal as well, though it should be concluded before sundown since Yom Kippur is a day of fasting from both food and drink. (Children and the sick are exempt from the fast.)

Rosh Hashana and Yom Kippur are the days when more Jews attend synagogue services than at any other time. Besides the prayers and Scripture lessons the service on Rosh Hashana includes the blowing of the *shofar* (ram's horn), which has been used since biblical times to assemble the people for great or sacred occasions. At the conclusion of Yom Kippur the shofar is blown again to signify that the fast is over, and those present are bidden, "Go, eat your bread with joy and drink your wine with happy heart, for God has accepted your works."

Five days after Yom Kippur, the feast of Tabernacles (Sukkot) is celebrated for eight days. Like Rosh Hashana and Yom Kippur, the first and last days of Sukkot are days of abstention from work, but during the middle days work may be done. In addition to attending services in the synagogue, traditional Jews construct a *sukka* (hut) near their homes in which to eat their meals during the holiday. The feast of Sukkot is the festival of thanksgiving for the harvest, while the *sukka,* built as a temporary abode in the fields during the harvest in ancient times, is symbolic of the fragility of life. The last day of the holiday is the most joyous of all, for at that time the scrolls of the Torah are paraded through the synagogue and the perpetual reading of Scripture is begun anew with the story of creation from the first chapter of Genesis.

Hanukkah is the celebration of the victory of the Maccabees over the oppressors who had desecrated the Temple and prohibited Jewish observances during the second century B.C.; it is observed for eight days during December, at or near Christmastime. It is primarily a home holiday when candles are lit each night to commemorate the victory of the few over the many and the rededication of the Temple to the worship of God. It is very much a children's holiday and, under the influence of the Christmas season, it has become a gift-giving time.

Purim is celebrated in February or March. This is the carnival holiday based on the book of Esther in the Bible. Similar to Mardi Gras, it is a time of masquerades and satire against authority. Children are very much involved in the festivities, and adults are even encouraged to get mildly drunk.

One month after Purim, near the time of the spring equinox, Passover (*Pesah*) begins. The Passover is, like the New Year and Day of Atonement, widely observed, even by Jews who are not that religiously involved on the other sacred days. It is one week long, with abstention from work on the first and last days. It is the season commemorating the exodus from Egypt and the liberation of Israel from bondage. Traditional Jews cleanse their houses thoroughly during the days prior to Passover, taking special care to eliminate all traces of leavened food, even crumbs, from the premises. For the entire week of the holiday no leavened bread or other leavened products may be eaten. The most prominent observance of the festival, however, takes place on the first two nights. This is when families gather together to celebrate the Seder, the narration of the story of the exodus and the festive meal accompanying it. Matzah (unleavened bread), called "the bread of affliction," must be eaten, along with some bitter herb, usually horseradish, as a reminder of the bitterness of slavery. Four glasses of wine are drunk to celebrate the four promises of redemption in Scripture, and the meal of lamb or other meat reflects the progression of Israel as a people and of each Jew individually "from bondage to freedom, from sorrow to joy, from darkness to great light."

Fifty days after the start of Passover the festival of Weeks or Pentecost (*Shabuot*) is celebrated. This is an old harvest festival that has also come to commemorate the giving of the Ten Commandments. The freedom made possible by the exodus only became real when the law of God was given. Linked to the Christian teaching that on Pentecost the "gift of tongues" descended upon the disciples is the older Jewish teaching that the Ten Commandments were given in all the languages of men.

DEVELOPMENTS IN MODERN JUDAISM

While Jewish life during the Middle Ages was not a history of unalloyed persecution, it is nonetheless true that neither in Europe nor in most countries of the Moslem world were Jews treated as full and equal citizens of the lands in which they lived. Small numbers of Jews settled early in the thirteen colonies that became the United States of America, but the true liberation of the Jews of Western and Central Europe did not occur until the French Revolution and the time of Napoleon. The French Revolution called for an end to all ethnic and religious distinctions as far as the rights of citizenship were concerned. Its watchword was "liberty, equality, and fraternity," and each person was to have a direct relationship with his country, not mediated through religious or communal institutions. The Jewish authorities in France proclaimed that every Jew was religiously bound to consider his non-Jewish fellow citizens as brothers and sisters, that he must aid, protect, and love them in the same measure as if they were Jews, that he must love the land of his birth or citizenship as his fatherland and defend it when called upon to do so. Thus the secular society came into being for the first time in history.

These developments gave rise to Reform Judaism in Germany during the first half of the nineteenth century. Reform Judaism was a movement of both rabbis and laymen who sought to adapt religion to the new conditions of the time. Jews for the first time in many centuries were able to receive a thorough secular education, and they were in search of a form of religious expression that would combine the heritage of the past with the culture of modern Europe. A scientific and historical approach to Scripture and other religious texts soon took hold in Reform circles, as it had among many Protestant scholars. Reform Judaism therefore was able to declare that many of the practices of the past were no longer obligatory. The dietary laws fell into disuse among most Reform Jews; some of the rules of Sabbath observance were modified; the synagogue service was no longer completely in Hebrew but vernacular languages were used as well; and women were granted the right to sit with men during worship and participate in the service on an equal level. Reform Judaism came to America soon after its development in Europe, and it was very influential in the integration of Jewish immigrants into American society and the American way of life.

Reform Judaism also eliminated the belief in the coming of a personal Messiah that is part of Orthodox teaching. In its place Reform emphasizes the hope for a "messianic age," when peace and human brotherhood will be the norm rather than the exception. Since the belief in a Messiah developed in an age when kings and emperors reigned, it was logical for the hope to grow that, as part of the redemption, a totally righteous king would reign over the world in place of the tyrannical rulers who had held sway. But when Reform Judaism was taking form, democracy was in the process of replacing autocratic monarchies, and the hope for a Messiah as "king of the world" had much less appeal than in ages past.

Likewise, Reform Judaism eliminated the belief in the bodily resurrection of the dead. A mistake that many Jews make about their own religion is in insisting that Judaism does not believe in the survival of the soul after death: "Christians believe in that; Jews don't." This is a misunderstanding of what Reform Judaism did. It eliminated only the belief in the resurrection of the body. It retained and even emphasized the life of the soul in the presence of God. What can be said accurately is that many Jews, as individuals, do not accept this teaching, preferring to believe that "when you're dead, you're dead." It is incorrect to say, though, that Judaism as a religious system ever denied the life of the soul after death.

The teaching of Judaism about the afterlife is very similar to that of Christianity. There is a difference in nuance, however. It probably is correct to say that many Christians, perhaps the majority, who participate in their religion do so because they believe in an after-life and want to be sure they will get there. This would not be true of Jews. Even Jews who believe in an afterlife, whether Orthodox, Conservative, or Reform, do not use this conviction as the basic motivation for their participation in religious worship or activity. Jews who are actively religious are that way because they believe this is their responsibility as human beings and as Jews, the descendants of Abraham, Isaac, and Jacob. The afterlife may be present as a reward, but this reward is not a motivation for their service of God.

Not all Jews embraced reform. Orthodox Judaism retains an allegiance to the Halacha, the system of Jewish law it regards as the revelation of God Himself to Moses, to the prophets, and to the authoritative rabbinic interpreters of every age. Orthodox synagogues conduct their services in Hebrew, and men are seated separately from women. Some Orthodox groups, such as the Hasidim ("pious ones"), preserve a distinctive mode of dress for both men and women, believing that it is desirable for Jews to segregate themselves from society in this way and that "modesty" in dress, particularly for women, is a requirement of the Halacha. Orthodoxy considers itself the only "genuine" Judaism. In earlier years in America Orthodoxy was not too prominent, but now that Orthodox Jews have achieved considerable success in both business and the professions, and speak as cultured an English as any other American, it has attained considerable stature.

Conservative Judaism began in Central Europe as a more moderate version of Reform. In America it helped to acculturate the millions of Jewish immigrants from Eastern Europe who arrived during the first half of the twentieth century. Many of them were looking for an alternative to Orthodoxy, but they did not feel comfortable in the Reform temples. In our own time there is not too much difference between the way of life of most Conservative and most Reform Jews. In the synagogue service, though, Conservative Judaism retains more Hebrew than Reform. It also stresses the dietary rules, though with a lesser emphasis on detail than the Orthodox. In recent years Conservative Judaism has emphasized the religious equality of men and women. Like Reform Judaism, it has begun to ordain women as rabbis, and because of this it has incurred the ire of many Orthodox authorities.

Reconstructionist Judaism is a smaller group than the others. An offshoot of Conservative Judaism, it was founded in America during the 1930s and embraces a very liberal theology, rejecting "supernaturalism" but insisting on retaining as much Jewish ritual as possible, not because these rites are the commandments of God but because they are Jewish "folkways" that preserve the distinctive culture of the people.

Here is how the three major groups of Jews might react to the challenge of eating in a non-kosher restaurant. A truly Orthodox Jew would not go, but if he could not avoid joining the group, he would content himself with a glass of water or a cup of coffee because the dishes on which food would be served would not be

33

kosher. A Conservative Jew would likely order a full meal but take care not to order any meat that was prohibited by the dietary regulations in the Torah. A Reform Jew would likely be willing to eat anything on the menu if it appealed to his personal taste.

The three groups also have distinctive ways of dealing with the wearing of the *yarmulke* (skullcap) that tradition recommends for Jewish men. The Orthodox Jew wears it at all times, both because it is a sign of modesty toward God, who is above, and because it is a public affirmation of Jewish identity. The Conservative Jew would be careful to wear it at worship or when reading a sacred Hebrew text but would take it off at other times. Most Reform Jews would not feel the need to wear it at any time (unless, of course, they were in an Orthodox or Conservative institution where they would conform to their custom).

Just as all Jews did not embrace Reform as a response to the emancipation the French Revolution brought to Central Europe, so too were many non-Jews unwilling to embrace the ideals of the revolution and regard the Jews as their brothers and sisters. Doctrines of romantic nationalism speaking of "blood and soil" took root in Central Europe, and even in France itself, as a reaction against the liberal and egalitarian ideas brought by the revolution, and "anti-Semitism" was born during the latter part of the nineteenth century. The world has always known "anti-Judaism," ideas in opposition to the teachings of the religion of Judaism, but anti-Semitism was something else. Anti-Semitism originally meant not only opposition to the Jewish religion but also the belief that there is something inherently noxious and evil in Jewish blood and that Jews by their very presence act as a corrupting influence on the peoples and cultures of the lands in which they live. Even conversion to Christianity could not save a Jew from the enmity of the anti-Semite.

The Jewish response to anti-Semitism was Zionism, the political and cultural movement that maintained the Jews would never find true acceptance anywhere in the world except in their own homeland. Zionism taught that the only way in which Jews could escape persecution was by returning to the ancestral homeland—Zion, the land of Israel (then known as Palestine). The first Zionist Congress, with delegates from most of the countries of Europe in which Jews lived, took place in 1897. Most of the Jews of Europe and practically all of the Jews in America rejected the Zionist message, however, keeping faith with the ideals spread by the French and American revolutions and looking toward the day when "liberty, equality, and fraternity" would become a reality everywhere. Very few Jews took up the opportunity of emigrating to Palestine.

In 1933 the Nazi party took control in Germany, and in a few years World War II was unleashed. Nazism was the direct outgrowth of the anti-Semitic movements in Central Europe. It took seriously the doctrines of anti-Semitism and quite logically, from its own point of view, embarked on a program of exterminating the Jewish people in the countries over which it had control. This attempt at extermination, or genocide, which resulted in the murder of six million Jews (out of a total worldwide population of fifteen million), has become known as the Holocaust. It is the single most traumatic event in the history of the Jews for the past two thousand years, and no Jew in the world who has any acquaintance at all with the heritage of his people can be unaffected by it.

The Holocaust gave new life to Zionism, and Jews throughout the world, including America, rallied to the cause of a Jewish homeland in Palestine. Many of those who were rescued from the death camps at the end of the war sought to make their new life in Palestine rather than remain in the charnel house that was Europe. When the British withdrew their forces from Palestine, the leaders of the Jewish community there proclaimed the birth of the State of Israel. The date was May 14, 1948. Just as no Jew can remain unaffected by the Holocaust, so can no Jew (or only very few) remain unaffected by the State of Israel. It represents the resurrection of a people. It is a replay of the story of Passover—the emergence of the people out of slavery into a new life. Jews throughout the world, while owing no political allegiance to Israel, take pride in its achievements and seek its peace and well-being.

The influence of the Holocaust and the birth of Israel has been felt by both religious and nonreligious, or secular, Jews. Not all Jews have a tie to synagogues and religious institutions. Many are members of secular Jewish organizations, such as Zionist groups, or cultural associations. Many are not members of any Jewish organization but still feel themselves tied to the people. Such people often say, "I am not a religious but a 'cultural' Jew." They are every bit as "Jewish" as those who attend synagogue every day since they sense and preserve the memory of descent from Abraham, Isaac, and Jacob, and are bound by bonds of blood and memory to the history and destiny of their people.

Because Judaism is rooted in the conviction that

the Jewish people constitute what is, in effect, an "extended family," it follows that marriage and family feeling play a large role in the Jewish consciousness. Husbands and wives are expected to show the utmost consideration to each other in all aspects of the marriage relationship. Because a serene and loving family atmosphere is so prized, divorce is permitted if the alternative would be constant turmoil and strife within the home. Sexual relations are not merely the means of bringing children to birth; they also serve as a way for husband and wife to give pleasure to each other and deepen their mutual love. Abortion is not considered equivalent to murder, though it is frowned upon except in cases when it is necessary for life or health. Various forms of birth control are practiced by most Jewish families, though Orthodox Judaism encourages its adherents to have as many children as they reasonably can expect to handle.

Children are treasured in Jewish families as the greatest of God's gifts. This is at the root of the great attention that is paid, sometimes to the point of extravagance, to the Bar Mitzvah celebration. This marks the coming of age of a Jewish boy, at or near his thirteenth birthday. The Hebrew term means that the young man is now ready to take on the observance of God's commandments (*Mitzvah*). The corresponding term for a girl is Bat Mitzvah. Parents sometimes prepare parties on these occasions that rival weddings and overshadow the importance of the religious ceremony itself. While this is often criticized in Jewish circles, it may reflect the great love and pride the parents share in their children and the joy they wish to share with family and friends. If this is the case, and the parents can afford a nice party, then perhaps they should not be chastised too severely.

The vast majority of Jews in America and Western Europe during this last part of the twentieth century, while feeling a tie to the land of Israel, do not look upon it as their "homeland." The "homeland" is the country in which they live and in whose culture they participate as full and equal citizens. It is for this reason many Jews see nothing wrong with interreligious marriage. Though Halacha, traditional Jewish law, forbids it, these people do not live by Halacha in other aspects of their lives and so see no reason to be bound by seemingly illogical prohibitions concerning whom they should or should not marry. Statistics are hard to come by, but it seems that close to fifty percent of American Jews are involved at some time or another with an interreligious marriage. The future will show if Judaism can survive the challenges of freedom as well as it has the challenges of adversity.

3

WHAT A JEW SHOULD KNOW ABOUT CHRISTIANITY

Christianity would not exist were it not for Judaism. Jesus of Nazareth was born, lived, and died a Jew. That he was believed to be the Messiah, the Christ for Christians, stemmed from the historic longing for a Messiah among the Jews of Jesus' time. A "Savior," another word Christians use for Messiah, could not communicate or function among a people who did not yearn for such a gift from God. Of course, Christians and Jews mean something far more than simple political and personal freedom when they speak of Christ or Messiah. It invokes a vision of a "new age" of fulfillment for all of creation. For both, the roots of that longing are buried deeply in Jewish history. Christianity was cradled in the faith and culture of Judaism.

Once some people began to express faith in Jesus as the Messiah, the two faiths with common origins began to move apart. The overwhelming majority of the Jews did not respond to and probably never even heard of Jesus during his lifetime. Christianity, while converting a significant number of Jews in its first century, grew as well among the many religious cults that flourished in the Roman Empire.

Paul, a converted Jew, recorded and helped guide the growth of the Christian faith in numerous letters, the oldest writings included in the Christian Scriptures. Four other books, called Gospels (Matthew, Mark, Luke, and John), tell the oral traditions that grew up specifically about the life of Jesus of Nazareth. These letters and books, called the New Testament, make up the second half of the Christian Scriptures. They tell the story sacred to Christians of the birth of Jesus at Bethlehem, on which the Christmas celebration is based, and his life as a traveling rabbi teaching service to and love of neighbor, peace, and justice in a new reign of God. They recall his journey to Jerusalem when he was approximately thirty-three years old, where he challenged the current religious authority. There he shared a final meal with his followers (which became the basis of Holy Communion), was arrested, tried, convicted of advocating rebellion, and put to death by crucifixion on Good Friday. According to the scriptural record Jesus was seen alive and well (the Resurrection) three days later on the first day of the week, Easter Sunday. The remainder of Christian Scriptures, the Old Testament, is identical to Hebrew Scriptures.

Much of what happens in church will be familiar to anyone nurtured in temple or synagogue traditions. Christian worship began there. More than two thirds of Christian Scriptures are easily recognized by Jews.

The service is in the language of the worshipers. No Hebrew is spoken or sung. Usually Christians who learn Hebrew are scholars and clergy who use it primarily for the study of Scripture. The New Testament books were written in Greek, but that language, too, is utilized mainly for Bible study.

The prayers are similar to those of the synagogue except for the almost universal Christian conclusion to prayer that is a variation on ". . . in Christ's holy name," just before the "Amen." Christians affirm Jesus Christ as the way they know and approach God; in almost every service they pray the "Lord's Prayer," also known as the "Our Father." Jesus taught this prayer to his followers, but any Jew should not hesitate to say the prayer. In fact, Jesus was sharing a traditional Hebrew prayer. Many other parts of Christian worship, including the use of hymns to praise God and the sermon (usually based on Scripture reading), all stem from Jewish sources.

SACRED CHRISTIAN RITUALS

In Christian worship nearly every tradition affirms at least two sacred acts (Catholics have seven), called sacraments, as central to the faith: Baptism and the Eucharist. These also have Jewish origins. In Jewish history baptism has at various times been performed as an act of purification related to ancient covenants. In Christianity baptism very early became the primary act of obedience through which an individual became a Christian and a member of the Church. It is always preceded by an affirmation of faith that Jesus Christ is Lord, God's Son, either by the candidate or, if he or she is a small child, by a parent or other person responsible for the child's rearing. Valid baptisms are always performed with water, and the candidate may be immersed or have water poured or sprinkled over the head.

In the baptismal service and also in many Christian prayers there are several names for God. The person administering the sacrament of Baptism, usually but not always an ordained clergy person, verbalizes that the sacrament is performed "in the name of the Father, Son, and Holy Spirit," three expressions or roles of God that Christians identify in Scripture. Father is the name given to the creator role of God who made all that exists. Son is the name for the role of Jesus Christ, the redeemer of humanity. Holy Spirit is the sustaining presence of God in all of life. Each is a facet of the one God, and the three facets make up the Trinity. Christianity is a monotheistic faith, as is Judaism.

Parents who wish their child to be nurtured in the Christian faith should know that Baptism is integral to entering the Christian community. Baptisms are often scheduled at special seasons, and Jewish people are always welcome. In addition to the parents of the baptismal candidate, often other family members and friends are present. A widely practiced tradition is for the parents to invite other family or close friends to act as godparents for their child. The godparents covenant to help nurture their godchild, especially in the faith of the child's parents. If the parents of the child should die while the child is in his or her early years, it is traditional for godparents to assume the parent role or be involved in determining who does. Because in many traditions those who act as sponsors and godparents must affirm their own Christian faith as well as covenant to nurture the baptismal candidate in the Christian faith, it is often impossible for people of other faiths to take these roles. In some churches the tradition is more open than in others, but a Jewish person asked to be a godparent for a Christian child should ascertain just what is expected by the family and the church in which the child will be reared. Should this create a problem in an interfaith marriage, many other creative and significant ways are available to Jewish family members and friends to participate meaningfully with integrity, if it is decided to nurture a child of an interfaith marriage in the Christian tradition.

Baptism usually is accompanied, sometimes years later, by another rite (or in the Roman Catholic Church, a sacrament) called Confirmation, in which a Christian is confirmed in faith and becomes a full member of the church. Confirmation, similar to the Bar Mitzvah in Jewish tradition, is the rite by which a child affirms that he or she has become a mature person able to support his or her own faith. It is preceded by a period of study and reflection. The Confirmation service includes a statement of faith in Christ as God's Son and an assurance that the candidate is aware of the basic tenets of the Christian faith. In some traditions it is accompanied by the candidate's First Communion. Gifts are often bestowed on the individual at this time, although it is rarely invested with the celebrative activity

Bar Mitzvah receives in Judaism. Whole families are often present for the services because of its significance. Adult Christian converts in almost every denomination are also required to receive Confirmation in addition to Baptism to become full members of the Church.

The other of the two sacraments in Protestant churches is the Eucharist (also called Holy Communion), a symbolic feast of thanksgiving. In most settings the reception of Communion has a holy and mystical quality with elaborate rituals, but in some traditions it is rather simple and straightforward. During the service worshipers recall the whole of Christ's life, especially emphasizing Jesus' final meal with his followers, his Crucifixion and Resurrection. It is the central drama of Christian worship. Worshipers experience a vivid remembering so that the feast becomes a reenactment of death and Resurrection, and in the act of remembering they experience the reality of Christ's presence. Bread, recalling Christ's body, and wine, recalling Christ's shed blood, are consecrated and served to dramatize the sacrificial gift of forgiveness and new life God bestowed upon the world in Christ. Following the confession of sins by all those who will receive Communion and an assurance of forgiveness, the priest, minister, or other ordained person engages in a liturgy of prayers of consecration and repeats words of institution, phrases that Jesus spoke at the Last Supper. He took bread, blessed it and broke it, and said, "This is my body. As often as you eat this bread, do it in remembrance of me." The cup is also shared in many traditions. The key word is "remembrance." Participation in this rite is for Christians an affirmation of God's holy spirit present and participating in the life of the world today. It is the sacramental act most often celebrated in Christian worship and, with the exception of certain Protestant traditions, is the center of most Christian services of worship.

Even this act so dear to Christian people the world over has Jewish origins. Scriptural tradition affirms that the Last Supper of Jesus with his followers before his death, where he instituted this sacrament, was probably a Passover meal, a Seder celebrated by Jesus with his friends. The link was surely made by the Gospel writers to tie Jesus to his Jewish heritage. The celebration of the Eucharist remembering Christ is for Christians similar in many ways to what the Passover remembering is for Jews. The divine covenant of liberation in the Passover story, which is sacred to Judaism, finds renewed confirmation for Christians in the celebration of Communion.

Many different interpretations are affirmed among Christians about the meaning of the Eucharist experience. An individual's interpretation often is related to the particular Christian tradition in which that person was nurtured and reared. While Jews are welcome at Eucharistic services, from both a Jewish and Christian point of view it is not appropriate for a non-Christian to receive Communion. It is assumed that those receiving the Eucharist share a common faith in Christ.

Why do Christians worship on Sunday? Isn't the biblical Sabbath the seventh day of the week, not the first? Or did Christians rewrite Scripture? No, the Sabbath was never changed from Saturday, but tradition affirms that Jesus' Resurrection occurred on a Sunday, now called Easter Sunday. Since every celebration of

Communion is a celebration of Easter, Sunday has become the traditional day of worship. Catholics sometimes participate in the Mass on Saturday evening, which reflects the Hebrew tradition that the new day begins not at midnight but at sundown the previous afternoon.

VARIETIES OF CHRISTIANS

Jews, who usually have to sort out among only three different Hebrew traditions, Orthodox, Conservative, and Reform, find it mystifying to differentiate among the varieties in Christianity, especially American Christianity. Three large families contain most Christians, but within some of those families the differences proliferate. The main faith families are Catholic, Protestant, and Orthodox. Within each family ethnic, sociological, cultural, and theological traditions add to the diversity. Traditions commonly affirmed by most Christian churches have been described in earlier portions of this chapter. One can hardly be a generic Christian, however; to be Christian means to belong to a particular Church tradition. While the traditions of Roman Catholics, many Protestants, and the Orthodox have been moving in recent decades toward more cooperation and mutual understanding, basic differences continue.

The two great families of Christians in Western Europe and the Americas are the Roman Catholics and the Protestants, from which many denominations have emerged since the Reformation in the sixteenth century. For nearly two thousand years the Catholic Church

46

has maintained and spread its Christian tradition and constantly developing practice of faith throughout the world. Modern Protestantism dates one of its beginnings from October 1517, when the German Catholic monk Martin Luther posted his famous "Ninety-five Theses" on the church door in Wittenberg. The reasons for the split between Catholics and Protestants are many, but they can be grouped into two areas: culture/piety and theology/church concerns.

Theologically the Catholic Church developed an understanding of faith and a hierarchical community at the fifth-century Council of Chalcedon, where early church practice and the developing Christian Scriptures were refined in the philosophical traditions of Plato and Aristotle and influenced by the political model of the late Roman Empire. The writings of the early church fathers of the East and West were cherished for their insights into faith and practice. Modern Catholic theology reached a peak in the writings of Thomas Aquinas (1225–1274). Very early in the Church's life the Eucharist (Mass) became the central expression of Christian worship.

During the centuries many other practices emerged in Catholic piety. From the age of chivalry, the Virgin Mary, mother of Jesus, took on a significant place in the lives of Catholics in a far more popular role than her place in Scriptures. The Rosary Prayer was developed, and many great cathedrals of Europe, such as Notre Dame and Chartres in France, built in her honor. Over the years martyrs and saints also became objects of devotion and intercession in the piety of Catholics.

Through the centuries different groups of men and women founded religious orders. Living a common life in monasteries and convents by taking vows of poverty, chastity, and obedience, they dedicated themselves to the spiritual life through contemplation. Others dedicated themselves to specific religious service: charity, education, and healing. While some groups and pious practices have come and gone, many of these traditions became precious elements of the religious life of Catholic Christians. By the fifteenth century these developments had added many layers of tradition to the original practices of Jesus' apostles and the early Church.

The leaders of the Protestant Reformation had as their primary goal the recovery of Scripture as the primary source of authority and practice in the Christian community. Practices that had developed since the early church period would not necessarily be abandoned, but, as the reformers contended, they should be critically evaluated from the Scriptural perspective. Most early Protestant leaders had little desire to eliminate Catholic traditions, such as the Mass, but wanted only to reclaim their Scriptural roots and eliminate what they felt were unsound accretions.

In practice, however, enmity grew between the two differing groups, and for nearly four centuries Catholic and Protestant Christians were engaged in an often bitter struggle for the loyalties of faithful people. Protestants toppled statues of saints and martyrs, decried the faithfulness of Catholics to the Virgin Mary, and were especially opposed to papal claims of divine authority as Vicar of Christ in the world. Tradition (including the authority of the Pope) over against the primacy of Scripture became the major contention. A counter-Reformation emerged in the Catholic Church determined to stamp out any unorthodox thought. The Catholic Inquisition and Protestant heresy trials represent the darkest period in history of enmity between the two traditions. In point of fact, Catholics were not all as neglectful of Scripture as Protestants claimed, nor were all Protestants as iconoclastic toward tradition as Catholics believed, but this made little difference in a climate of stereotype and prejudice. Despite all of this, the faithful lives of millions of Christians all over the world continued to flourish.

During the sixteenth century other major contentions contributed to the schism: the breaking down of monarchy, the emergence of new national consciousness, and the development of representative governments. Protestantism, with few exceptions, emerged as the champion of the individual and shared authority, holding to Scripture as the arbiter of revealed truth. The Catholic Church responded to these developments through a hierarchical church order. It maintained and preserved its differences in response to Protestant reformers and changes. Through the Council of Trent, the Catholic Church solidified its spiritual practices and legal traditions. Its leanings toward monarchy reinforced the Pope's powers as a temporal ruler and his role as the "first among equals" of the bishops of the world. The Pope is traditionally looked upon as the successor to St. Peter, who is believed to have been the first Bishop of Rome.

Because the New Testament focused on one community of faith, it was necessary for each group to maintain that it was the true and right church, thus the one Church. Each accused the other of heresy. The piety of this period of history included an important dimension that to many appears presumptuous and often irrelevant today; that is, one achieved "favor with God" and immortality through the "right" confession of faith, creedal statement, and/or completion of a particular set of actions. Catholics and Protestants were seriously discouraged from fraternizing, and marriage between a Catholic and a Protestant became anathema to both traditions. Between certain Protestant groups the enmity was almost as strong. Most claimed the truth of their particular interpretation of Scripture and/or tradition. Most rejected or excommunicated any who strayed from their understanding of orthodoxy.

The twentieth century has seen major steps toward reconciliation between Protestants and Catholics and also among the Protestant denominations. Today the Catholic Church again emphasizes the major importance of Scripture. Protestants are rediscovering the sacredness of two thousand years of Christian tradition. Many cordial and mutually reconciling dialogues between Catholics and Protestants are in progress throughout the world. Christians of many backgrounds joyfully celebrate their faith and share a common commitment to peace, justice, and human liberation. But among the remaining differences, one stands out: church order; that is, the difference between a magisterial model of the Church symbolized by the authority and teaching power of the Vatican and the Pope in the Catholic tradition and the shared authority of clergy and laity that is the hallmark of Protestantism.

Within Christianity, loyalties to particular streams of faith are changing. The Catholic Church at the Second Vatican Council (1965) recognized the validity of other churches in preserving the Christian faith, but

Catholics seem in general to be far more loyal to their particular tradition than are Protestants. Protestants will sometimes change denomination as they move from one community to another, primarily because of convenience (no parish of their particular church is nearby), or because they find a congregation of another denomination with which they feel more at home. Mutual recognition of one another's members makes such a change relatively easy to make. Marriage between Protestants and Catholics still raises questions in a few traditions, but neither the Catholic Church nor any mainline Protestant group actively opposes such a union. A growing sense of reconciling trust between mainline Protestants and Catholics in the United States, Canada, and Western Europe is breaking down prejudice and discovering common ground for faithful response to the Christian gospel. These developments have also opened new possibilities for Jewish-Christian relationships as trust replaces suspicion and stereotype in peoples' lives.

Catholic Christianity

Most Jews in America are familiar with the Catholic Church's existence and some of its practices, probably because it is the largest Christian denomination in the U.S. and because both Jews and Catholics have large memberships concentrated in major urban areas. The two groups have rubbed elbows for a long time, and sometimes even more than that. The contact is mostly external, even at times warm and charming. (Many older Catholics have reminiscences of receiving a penny or a nickel to turn on lights and stoves for Jewish neighbors on the Sabbath and to this day are mystified and edified by Sabbath observances.)

Without being able to remove most of the mysteries, the information in this chapter should explain some workings of the Roman Catholic Church.

TRADITION: The Catholic Church, unlike some Christian denominations in America, is an international body of believers with very strong Western European roots and traditions. The prominence of Rome as its center dates from early times when Christianity spread throughout the Mediterranean. While the city grew in prominence as the center of the empire, it evolved as the center of the Catholic Church.

The development of the Catholic Church in America was influenced by the early colonizers: Spanish in the West (California) and South (Florida), the French in Louisiana, Canada, and the Northeast, as well as English settlers (notably in Maryland). But the growth and development of the Catholic Church were very modest, and most early missionary efforts were not very successful. Not until the nineteenth century, when waves of Irish, German, and Italian immigrants arrived, was the Catholic Church shaped the way we are familiar with it today. The development followed the assimilation of the immigrants into the new land and its major institutions; cathedrals, parish churches, schools, universities, hospitals, and social services flow from that era, not its early missionary efforts. The Catholic Church in America can be said to be a relatively recent development. As a structure it is now tied to the status of the United States in general. It still reflects "old-new" world cultural tensions of immigrant America.

Reflecting these developments, it has produced the "rare birds" called American Catholics.

If there is an old and a new culture in America from its immigrant days, Catholicism shares in that dynamic: Its faith and practice as well as its development are intertwined with cultural overtones. That is one adjustment for the institution. For couples planning a marriage it is another. First-generation Catholics in America have more complications than third-generation immigrants. This is not so much from faith as from cultural differences. The decisions concerning the place of the wedding, the food, the music, and how the ceremony is conducted sometimes have more to do with culture than with faith.

The Catholic Church attempts to blend its faith heritage into a particular cultural context. At a wedding you see a microcosm of that process for the vast international Church. The blending of belief in love, fidelity, permanence, children, and family life with its components in an organized international Church is an ongoing dynamic attempting to translate values and divine revelation to a contemporary cultural setting. The Catholic Church moves very slowly in those areas.

THEOLOGY: Catholic theology embraces a creed, code, and cult (ritual). What the Catholic Church believes is summarized in its creed, recited at Mass. The most common ones are called the Apostles Creed and the Nicene Creed (which are affirmed by many Protestant denominations as well). They uphold that God, who is the Creator, spoke at the dawn of time and continued to speak through the centuries, for example, to Abraham, Noah, Moses, and others, and one day God spoke through an angel to a woman, Mary. God's Word became a human being. So Catholics uphold Jesus as someone who *had* and *was* a message. In Himself or through His message, which is presented again through the body of believers, His Word, like all other language, evokes a response in the hearer. (If I should curse at someone, my words have evocative power.) And so does the Word of God, Catholics believe. They call this power the Holy Spirit and thus complete the Church's definition of God as He is and as He is experienced in the Trinity: a Father Creator, a Son who is the Word made flesh, and the Holy Spirit, the Word's grace continuing to call a person to an eternal relationship in His kingdom here and in the resurrected future. This is the central tenet of the Catholic faith: a God revealing himself as a triune God, with a Word made flesh for salvation and life.

CODE: Besides a creed, Catholicism embraces a code, the familiar Ten Commandments, as well as the two great ones repeated by Jesus: love of God and love of neighbor (a code embraced by all Christians). Contrary to popular impressions, commandments are not recipes or guides to good conduct that ensure entrance to the pearly gates. They're a code that flows from what Catholics believe. Not stealing, for example, expresses faith in God's providence, not a fear of getting caught! Other commandments have similar values and beliefs at their root—justice, honor, prayer, and so forth. The other rules in the tradition come from the Catholic Church's canon law. It has evolved through the centuries to govern everyday practices and observances for the Church—to determine membership and its good order, and to outline rights, duties, responsibilities, jurisdiction, and accountabilities. The canons or laws of the Church are not rooted in the British common law tradition, so familiar to us as Americans, but have more to do with the Napoleonic code and a hierarchical structure. The Catholic Church's structure would be similar to that of the U.S. military: a chain of command with very few democratic procedures, such as voting, in its day-to-day operations. The Pope, bishops, curias (that is, chanceries—central offices and officers), and pastors of congregations (parishes) make up the chain of command from top to bottom. They are "in charge," or have jurisdiction over the faith and practice of the Church. With time, the canons are debated and studied by lawyers of the Church, and changes and revisions are made—usually slowly—to adjust to new circumstances. The latest revision was made in November 1984, after seventy years.

LITURGY: The third thing about Catholicism to be familiar with is its ritual, properly called its liturgy. It is composed of seven ceremonies (sacraments) and its official book of prayers (the Divine Office). Sometimes sacraments are stereotyped as similar to rites of passage, but in fact they are the Church's forms of worship, its acts of faith, public and private. The sacraments initiate a person into, as well as become the vehicles for sustaining members in, their spiritual and prayer lives. Some of the sacraments are seen as highly personal, such as Penance (confession), Anointing the Sick, Baptism, and Confirmation. Some are more public social actions that are corporate, as in the Eucharist; but strictly speaking, they are actions of the whole Church wherever and whenever they are celebrated. (One would need another book to elaborate on the metaphysics and cosmology that are the philosophical bases of explaining these aspects of the Church's spiritual life.) The sacrament of Matrimony celebrates the covenant of God's love and is the only one not conferred by a priest. While he serves as the official witness for the Church, the bride and groom confer the sacrament on each other. The seventh sacrament is Holy Orders (ordination to the priesthood).

The use of the Bible is extensive in Catholic rituals, especially during the Mass. A three-year cycle of readings from the Scriptures (also utilized by many Protestant denominations) draws from every book of the Bible.

The last element of the liturgy is the calendar. A common calendar followed by nearly all Christians concludes this chapter. In addition to the celebrations described there, the Catholic Church also includes celebrations in honor of the Blessed Virgin Mary and those holy men and women (saints) who are distinguished and recognized for their practice of the faith throughout the centuries. Today these celebrations are not as prominent as they once were in the devotions of the Church, though they are still present.

The calendar is a logical place to see the focus of devotion to Mary, the Blessed Mother of Jesus. Though the months of May and October are times for special private devotions, her place in the life of the Church is seen more easily in relation to the way the Church extols the events in her life in connection with the events in Christ's life. She serves as a model for us humans. She cooperated with God's grace in a unique way and becomes a "type" (to use a theological term) symbolizing the Church. When the whole Church tries to re-present the life of Christ in its efforts to make the Word flesh again in our age and culture, she becomes the model. In comparison with other religions, especially those in the East, she is more of an "earth mother," not a goddess or fertility symbol. She is a caring, nurturing, fruitful, and faith-filled model in a relationship with a God who is invisible and eternal.

Three of the "holy days of obligation," times when Catholics are required to be present at Mass, are centered about the Blessed Virgin. One is December 8, the Feast of the Immaculate Conception. This does not commemorate the virgin birth of Christ but rather the conviction that, as the mother of God, Mary enjoyed favor and grace and was free from sin from the moment of her conception. On January 1, the Solemnity of Mary, Mother of God, is celebrated. August 15 is the Feast of the Assumption of Mary, celebrating the conviction that she rose body and soul into heaven.

Besides the three holy days of obligation centering upon Mary, there are three other days during the year, other than Sundays, when Catholics are required to be present at Mass. One is Christmas. The second is the Ascension, falling on the Thursday forty days after Easter. This celebrates the ascent of Christ into heaven. The third is All Saints' Day on November 1. This is a day of remembrance for all the faithful, ordinary folk as well as those whose names and careers are well known, who have struggled to make holiness a reality during ages past. Halloween, which has lost its religious significance for most people, falls on October 31 because it is the eve of All Saints' (once called All Hallows) Day.

Some features of Catholic churches are found in Protestant churches as well. Especially prominent in all churches are a pulpit and an altar. The altar is the site of the sacrifice of Christ (Good Friday) and the site of his sacred meal of the new covenant (Holy Thursday). In Catholic churches there is also a tabernacle where Communion wafers are reserved for the sick and as an object of devotion. Their presence is signified by a special red lamp, and the tabernacle is situated usually at or near the main altar, or in another prominent place.

Some modern churches are considered cold and impersonal, and are replete with abstract design. They emphasize that the mystery of Christ is not represented until a congregation is present that affirms God's presence in the midst of a faithful people who hear, listen, and act on His word. Other churches are cozy devotional places with many representational images, highlighting the personal relationship a person has to God and Christ. Such structures are usually filled with candles, representational stained glass, and images of saints to edify and inspire those who come to pray, and remind them of their own unique relationship to God.

No matter what the century or theological emphasis, the Cross or Crucifix has a prominent and central place in every church, Catholic, Protestant, and Orthodox. Some buildings are even built in the form of a cross, which represents many things. Its prominence is not a call to misery, suffering, and pain, however, but represents a symbolic call to the way of salvation. The Scriptures are filled with the symbols of God's promise of salvation. God manifested the rainbow to Noah, a word of fruitfulness to Abraham, and the burning bush to Moses. For Catholics, as for nearly all Christians, the wooden Cross, recalling the Tree of Life, is the ultimate sign that God will be faithful to His promise and live with His people by sharing and even surrendering His life. Catholics do not believe that Christ merely suffered ignominy and died for us on the Cross. They believe that he lived and surrendered his life to reveal the invisible and eternal God who shares His life with humanity—true to the revelation of Christ who called Him his Father.

The space and the symbols in a church reveal the mystery of the way Catholics believe God acts. To suffer and die is not a mindless and needless act. The meaning of Christ's death is that he offered his life as a gift for others, for he knew its true value. Life is not to be saved, to be protected as in a safe deposit box, but is to be used as a great gift that will disclose the value and dimension of each human being.

This is one reason Catholics consider marriage so important and a holy sacrament. When the gift of life is freely and generously offered, it becomes once again a sign of God's presence in our world. It unlocks the future. A husband and wife united with God in this world reveal His kingdom in our midst.

Perhaps the Catholic Church can best be understood as a highly organized, multicultural, historical body of believers with Christ at its core and center. Its code, and to some extent its creeds and liturgy, distinguishes it historically as different from but not better than other Christian churches.

Protestant Christianity

Protestants and Catholics, as far as the basics of faith are concerned, share a common heritage. Though Protestant worship may appear very different from the Catholic Mass, it has in it the same elements and traditions. But there are, of course, major differences.

Scores of churches have emerged since the Protestant Reformation of the sixteenth century. Many of the issues that caused the separation are no longer as divisive. The major concern had to do with the Protestant commitment to a larger role and voice for the laity (non-clergy). A major Protestant affirmation is "the priesthood of all believers." Most Protestant churches have a democratic or representative form of structure where the laity share authority with the clergy. Other issues as well as political loyalties were involved. America's first European settlers were made up primarily of Protestant groups. Many of them trace their origins back to movements in particular nations or states, but in America, and even in Europe, these groups no longer serve exclusively the people of a particular national heritage. Since 1960 Protestant denominations have been increasingly in cooperation and dialogue with the Roman Catholic Church. The ecumenical movements of the twentieth century have helped to break down many barriers and have given many a wider appreciation of the common faith shared by all Christians.

We will confine ourselves to the so-called mainline Protestant groups and other churches that are significant because of the size of their membership. Most Protestant churches accept interfaith marriages. Only a minority of clergy among some of the groups discussed below would actively oppose an interfaith marriage.

In describing the varieties of Protestantism we will limit our discussion to those dimensions that have implications for interfaith relationships. The major groups within Protestantism can be understood by their approach to the culture about them. Mainline Protestant churches do not usually reject the culture in which they live; they may seek to make changes in it rather than remove themselves from it. In the past century they have learned to live rather comfortably in a pluralistic society. Members of these churches take their faith seriously and are concerned with issues of peace, justice, and compassion, but their traditions include a healthy respect for persons of other faith traditions. The major Protestant churches in this category include the Episcopal Church (which retains more Catholic practices than other denominations), the United Methodist Church, the Presbyterian Church, the United Church of Christ, the Christian Church (Disciples of Christ), most of the Lutheran churches, the American Baptist Church, the United Church of Canada, and some smaller denominations.

The names borne by some of these groups may seem a bit strange to those unfamiliar with Church history. The Episcopal Church, which began as the American mission of the Church of England, is so called because it retains an "episcopal" form of church government, like Roman Catholicism. That is to say, each geographic district is governed by a bishop (from the Greek *episkopos,* bishop or overseer). The Presbyterian Church, on the other hand, is governed by councils of elders (from Greek *presbyteros,* elder). The Presbyterian tradition was heavily inspired by the work of the Swiss theologian John Calvin and by churches that grew up in Scotland and Holland. The Lutherans follow the teachings of Martin Luther and are numerous in Germany and Scandinavia. Baptists believe that infants are not qualified for Baptism, and that this sacrament of initiation should be received only by those old enough to understand and accept Christian doctrine. The Methodist Church began as a movement of reform within the Church of England during the eighteenth century, led by John and Charles Wesley. The name originally was a term of ridicule applied to those who strove to be very "methodical" in their religious devotions.

In general, Protestant churches look to Scripture as the primary source of authority. How they interpret Scripture says much about how they relate to people from other religious traditions. Most Protestant theology encourages individual responsibility and an educated approach regarding the interpretation of faith. Augustine's "faith seeking understanding" characterizes the Protestant pilgrimage of faith. Diversity of interpretation thrives. Acceptance of others usually is not based on their having the "right" answers to questions of faith.

The majority of Protestants cherish their ethnic and cultural heritages, but not as a way of separating one group from another. Many Protestants in America come from a particular national church with roots in Europe. Today, however, the Swedish and Danish Lutherans, who settled primarily in Minnesota and Wisconsin, the New England Congregationalists, Presbyterians, and Episcopalians from England, Scotland, and Wales have begun to blend into a larger community. The old divisions have given way in many instances to cooperative and united churches. This spirit of an emerging ecumenism (unity) has made possible a reaching across faith lines that could not have occurred a few generations back. Having already reached successfully across barriers within their own faith, an openness to the possibilities of interfaith relationships is growing. This is not to say that the barriers among Christians are comparable to those between Jews and Christians, but the possibilities of breaking them down are greater now than they were a half century ago.

Most Protestant traditions affirm that the whole inhabited earth is of God's community. A Jew, a Christian, a Muslim, a Hindu, each is God's own child. The differences to be bridged in most Protestant-Jewish marriages have to do with cultures, celebrations, and traditions, not questions of whose faith is valid or who is more or less acceptable to God.

While marriage is not designated a sacrament in the Protestant tradition, it is a sacred and holy covenant and not to be entered into unadvisedly or irreverently. Most Protestant clergy would be pleased to officiate at a Jewish-Christian marriage, after a period of counseling in which they assured themselves that each partner understood and respected the traditions of the other in the context of a caring, committed relationship.

SOME SPECIAL SITUATIONS: One group of Protestants affirm themselves as "fundamentalists" and take the position that the Bible is the inerrant as well as inspired word of God. Variety of opinion and interpretation is much less prevalent. It is important for these people to find one authoritatively correct answer to most questions of faith. Those who have been nurtured in this tradition would have genuine problems in an interfaith marriage because it would be very difficult for them to accept the validity of the faith or heritage of someone from a different tradition. Many of the Southern Baptist churches, the Churches of Christ (not the United Church of Christ), Pentecostal churches, a few individual Catholics, and many independent churches take this position. A Jewish person should enter into a relationship with an individual nurtured in a fundamentalist tradition with caution.

Fundamentalist Protestants occasionally have a hard time establishing close relationships with more liberal Protestants. In a similar vein, but for different reasons, a liberal Protestant may experience difficulties in a marriage to an Orthodox Jew. The liberal Protestant, whose approach to faith is more universally oriented and who has been nurtured since birth as a reconciler of differences, may be overwhelmed by the seeming rigidity of tradition that is cherished in Orthodox Judaism. The Protestant spouse and parent might experience frustration in seeking "via media" with an Orthodox Jewish partner whose heritage insists on a regular ritual of life that is far more prescriptive than the Protestant heritage. The matter can be especially complicated if a Christian wife and an Orthodox Jewish husband wish to rear their children in certain Orthodox Jewish traditions because the child's Jewish identification comes through the mother. Because individuals are dealing with unstated different life-styles that may not be revealed in any other dimension of their life together, the tension may not be overtly communicated. In addition, in-laws are often subtly drawn into such conflicts.

Another unlikely but nevertheless occasional occurrence is the marriage between a fundamentalist Christian and an Orthodox Jew. Because of the exclusiveness inherent in both traditions, this opens the way to conflict that should be addressed in a counseling setting long before marriage.

It may seem unlikely that fundamentalist Christians and Jews, or liberal Protestants and Orthodox Jews, would establish relationships. Often, however, differences of faith and religious heritage are not considered barriers until a major change occurs in the family or a child is born. Particularly because fundamentalist Christians make up a significant minority among American Christians and are a presence in almost every denomination, a Jewish individual should ask serious questions very early if the partner takes fundamentalist positions regarding faith. Many people with these backgrounds grow to be very accepting of people from different backgrounds, but it is often a difficult transition for them to make. Conversion, by one or the other party, may be the only option. Fundamentalists often feel, almost unwittingly, that they must convert people they care about to their faith position. To them it is a way to assure themselves that these persons are not "lost" and separated from God. (The authors must affirm that no judgment is implied about what faith position is right or wrong, only that for a fundamentalist Christian and a Jew to develop a relationship, either the Jew will need to convert or the Christian will need to discover another way to affirm his or her faith.)

A tangent of fundamentalism is another group within some Protestant and Catholic communities called charismatic Christians. Charismatic simply means spirit-filled, and both Judaism and Christianity have cherished traditions of charismatic figures—the great prophets of Hebrew tradition. The young Isaiah in the Temple, Jeremiah, Ezekiel, all were genuine charismatic figures. Pentecost, the conversion of Paul, the transfiguration of Jesus are examples of Christian charismatic experiences. Members of the charismatic movement among Christians today claim special gifts of the Holy Spirit that make it possible for them to experience the presence and activity of God in ways beyond rational experience. All religious persons would affirm that there is a mystery about faith which moves beyond the five senses, but the charismatics claim special gifts such as "speaking in unknown tongues," faith healing, and exotic "born again" experiences of the Holy Spirit in their lives. They are not always fundamentalists, but they do take seriously the rather isolated examples of spirit-filled group activity recorded in Scripture. The experience often can be traumatic and life-changing for the individual, sometimes helpful, other times destructive. One who is relating to a person claiming charismatic experience should be aware that charismatics often need their companions to share their charismatic experiences and sometimes relate to noncharismatics as if they were somehow less faithful persons. The only churches made up primarily of charismatics are the various Pentecostal congregations throughout the world, religious groups that are growing everywhere.

When love unites two people, one Jewish, the other a fundamentalist Christian, many possibilities of a good relationship are already present. The Christian has already admitted to himself or herself that the other individual is one in whom love and care can be invested. To love one of another tradition means certainly to be involved and interested in that individual's heritage. Counseling with an open clergy person who understands and is sympathetic to the fundamentalist position, but who can help the individual toward a broader approach, is important and should be pursued. However, such discussion must be approached with great care. It is usually fruitless to try to argue one's way through a disagreement about faith. Love conquers all—for a time—but deep-seated traditions that can set up barriers often arise much later in the marriage if they are not reconciled early in the relationship.

These special situations are not likely to be met by most interfaith couples. But when they are, it is always possible to find, among the Protestant community, clergy and congregations who are accepting of interfaith marriage. Diversity is a hallmark of Protestant traditions.

ORTHODOX CHRISTIANITY

In the Western Hemisphere a significant but comparatively small group of Christians affirm the ancient Orthodox Christian faith. In Russia, Greece, and the surrounding areas, almost every Christian has an Orthodox heritage. Like the Roman Catholic Church, Orthodox Christians trace their history to the beginnings of Christianity. Their tradition affirms the same sacraments affirmed by other Christian groups, but their development in a Byzantine culture gives their worship a feeling quite different from liturgies developed in the West. The Resurrection is the primary celebration in their services, and their art and architecture have a mystical quality that seeks to transcend time and space. It provides a rich and beautiful tapestry of religious experience that appears exotic to people nurtured in Western Christianity.

Because Orthodox Christians have often been isolated from and have not had long ties with the developing pluralism of the West, they tend to live in more closely knit communities than either Protestants or Catholics (although this is changing in an increasingly mobile society). As a result marriage between an Orthodox Christian and a Jew would be somewhat unusual and could present problems for an Orthodox Christian family, although it is not forbidden from an Orthodox point of view. Orthodox priests may share in officiating at interfaith marriages, but one should not presume that this is always the case. Orthodox understanding of authority is much more closely aligned with the Roman Catholic tradition than with the Protestant. The Orthodox churches are in dialogue with both the Roman Catholic and many Protestant churches. More open, accepting relationships are being established already.

AN OLD ENMITY REVISITED

At some point conversations may turn to the assumptions and concerns that have tended to build walls between Jews and Christians (Catholics, Protestants, and Orthodox) through the centuries. Many of these concerns never needed to emerge, although history is filled with the tragic results of religious misunderstandings that became a source of enmity. One area of contention between Jews and Christians stems from

68

statements that have in the past accused the Jews of being responsible for the crucifixion of Jesus. We cannot overlook the dark centuries when relationships between Jews and Christians were deeply hostile, when this issue was at the heart of a conflict that grew into a widening set of destructive prejudices. The single most tragic event of the twentieth century, the Holocaust, finds one of its roots in this ancient accusation. Such points of view are confined today to small, isolated groups who are rejected by mainline Christianity. For this tragic and sad era the Church and Christians need and seek the forgiveness of the Jewish community. Christians today increasingly recognize Jesus' Jewishness and emphasize that Jesus' death was the result of the universal human condition which, seemingly without fail, rejects the life people were divinely created to live. Jesus of Nazareth, to Christians, represented that divinely created life. That he was a Jew, and rejected by some of them, is an example of the universal rejection the world brings to such people. Every age has its martyrs; every religious heritage reveres those who gave their lives for the sake of cherished beliefs. Jesus' death is in that tradition. Faith in his Resurrection demonstrates that God's forgiveness and love transcend even that ultimate rejection and death.

Almost without exception, Christian ethical and moral principles are in agreement with those of Judaism. Differences may occur in working out the detailed principles, but the overarching counsel for justice, peacemaking, and loving and serving neighbors is the same in both faiths. Jesus' commandments to love God and neighbor were quotations from his own Jewish nurture in faith. While all Christians accept these principles, they respond to them in at least as many different ways as Jews respond in their tradition. The "Christian" or "Jewish" thing to do in ethical decision-making has more to do with an individual's understanding of the issue than with anything unique to one faith or the other.

THE NITTY-GRITTY: LOVE, MARRIAGE, AND SEX

Christianity and Judaism both hold marriage and the family in high esteem, affirming the physical and spiritual love of man and woman as one of the most joyful gifts of God, our Creator. Children are considered blessings to be nurtured, cherished, and loved. The faith of the parents is to be inculcated in their children. Any religious tradition is only one generation from extinction. If people fail to remember, a living heritage becomes a dead past. A family's heritage of faith and culture, more than anything else, helps the members of each generation remember and identify who they are. In marriage a hallowed tradition is to keep the family's religious heritage alive for future generations. This alone is reason enough for each member of an interfaith marriage to be familiar with the religious culture and heritage of the other.

Consideration of marriage will trigger questions about the way Christians view sex. Catholics and Protestants do not regard the purpose of sexual intercourse in the same way. Though both view sex in marriage as an affirmation of love and the mutual support of both spouses, the Catholic Church teaches that an equally

important purpose is the procreation of children. Protestants would agree except that for most of them sexual intercourse is an act that can be enjoyed without
regard to procreation. The Catholic point of view, however, is that nothing should be allowed to interfere
with the divinely ordered process of procreation. This
precludes the utilization of many medically accepted
methods of birth control and some sexual activities
outside of traditional sexual intercourse. Only certain
limited forms of birth control are permitted (usually
intercourse during times of the female cycle when fer-
tilization is not possible). Admittedly this position is
unpopular with some Catholics who are otherwise faithful. The Protestant view is that, while procreation is a
basic function of sexual activity, intercourse and sexual
play may be enjoyed within marriage as a simple affirmation of love and as an end in itself. Protestants are
encouraged to utilize any medically approved form of
contraception unless a child is desired.

The difference in approach also explains the distance between Catholic and Protestant responses to
abortion. Neither tradition views abortion as a recommended form of birth control. However, since in Catholic teaching one purpose of sexual intercourse is for
procreation, the Church expressly forbids abortion as a
direct attack on innocent fetal life. Some Protestants
agree, but most generally accept the compromise worked
out by the United States Supreme Court and affirm
that individual circumstances should govern the decision and that a woman should be able to responsibly
exercise her own will regarding the need for abortion
in the early months of pregnancy, when a good and
valid reason is apparent. In Protestant theologies early

abortion is not looked upon as an attack on innocent life. Our century has produced rapid changes in sexual practices, and many theologians and institutions are taking a long, hard look at human sexuality. Sex is a gift from God, but human definitions of the appropriate expressions of that gift are no longer as clear as they were just a few years ago. Even the definition of what makes up a family is in transition, although the concept of family is as cherished as ever.

Divorce is a fact of life in our society. Catholics and Protestants view marriage as a lifelong sacramental covenant between two persons and blessed by God. Various traditions have different responses, however, when a marriage ends in divorce. No mainline Protestant church forbids divorce or refuses to accept a divorced person into its communities. When given the opportunity, Protestant clergy will seriously counsel with people in a troubled marriage and seek to determine if reconciliation is possible. In cases where differences appear irreconcilable, the clergy at times may recommend separation or divorce as the only viable alternative. Protestants tend to view divorce with great regret and sorrow, as any broken sacred covenant, but not as a sin that cannot be forgiven or that would bar a Christian from the sacramental fellowship. The approach would not differ in an interfaith marriage. More conservative Protestants have particular practices regarding divorce and the acceptance of divorced persons that vary with the denomination.

Canon law in the Catholic Church is quite specific in not recognizing divorce as a religious procedure. Marriage is a sacrament, a covenant that must not be broken. A marriage can sometimes be annulled, though, meaning that in the Church's judgment a valid sacramental union never existed. Each diocese has within its structure a marriage tribunal which carefully investigates the requests for annulment that come before it. These investigations usually take a good bit of time, and not all the requests lead to the granting of an annulment. A Catholic who nonetheless receives a civil divorce remains in good standing within the Church unless he or she marries again without having received the Church's annulment of the original marriage. Someone who remarries without the annulment is not supposed to receive Communion.

It is important to note that the Church's attitude regarding the permanence of marriage extends not only to its own marriages but to those performed within other religions as well. Thus, if a Jew who had been married to another Jew in a Jewish ceremony got a divorce and subsequently wished to marry a Catholic, he or she would have to apply to the Church's marriage tribunal for an annulment of the original marriage.

Family life is as sacred to Christians as to Jews. Because Christianity has generally not defined itself as an ethnic tradition, the sense of the Christian community as a family heritage is not as strong as it is in Judaism. Nonetheless, parents, grandparents, and generations past are greatly revered by all Christians and play a large role in Christian family life. Christian pastors often counsel young couples who are preparing for marriage to remember that "you don't just wed each other but a whole new family." This brings particular joys and challenges to an interfaith marriage.

MAJOR CHRISTIAN HOLIDAYS

Many Christian holidays, like their counterparts in Judaism, are surrounded by community and cultural traditions that may have rather little to do with the historic or religious background of the celebration. Chapter 6 discusses the observance of religious holidays in the home, the family celebrations and traditions. Here we provide an outline of a yearlong calendar of the major Christian holidays.

Advent is the four-week period prior to Christmas (December 25). It is a season of preparation for Christmas, including self-examination. Often in churches and in homes an Advent wreath of four candles (three purple and one rose-colored) is lighted, with one candle being lit each Sunday as a way of counting the time and reminding the people that the "Light of the World" is soon to be born. The lighting of the candles is often accompanied by prayer and readings from Scripture or other sources.

Christmas is a celebration that can be concentrated on December 25 or extended for twelve days to Epiphany. It celebrates the birth of Christ, and gift-giving is traditional. Other traditions include decorated Christmas trees, crèche scenes, carol-singing, and special services in churches (especially on Christmas eve).

Epiphany celebrates the visitation of the wise men to adore the Christ child, twelve days after Christmas (January 6). In some cultures this is the time during the Christmas season when gifts are exchanged.

Ash Wednesday is the first day of **Lent**, a period of forty days (not counting Sundays) prior to Easter. It is a day of deep self-examination and penance, and in some traditions ashes are placed on the worshiper's forehead as a sign of that penance. Lent is the penitential season when one continues to prepare for the celebration of the Resurrection.

Holy Week is the last week of Lent. The week begins with Palm or Passion Sunday, celebrating Jesus' entry into Jerusalem. Some of the other special days during that week are Maundy or Holy Thursday, when the Eucharist was established by Jesus at the Last Supper with his disciples, and Good or Black Friday, the day of Jesus' crucifixion. Each of these days is commemorated with special services. On Saturday night some churches have an Easter vigil just prior to midnight to watch and wait for the arrival of Easter.

Easter Sunday is the great springtime Christian holiday, the celebration of the Resurrection of Christ. Easter is a movable feast; that is, it is celebrated according to a rather complicated lunar calendar, often coming near Passover. Churches often have their largest attendance of the year at Easter.

There are other observances less emphasized by individual Christians but important in the life of the churches. **Ascension**, forty days after Easter, celebrates Christ's ascent into heaven. **Pentecost** recalls the coming of the Holy Spirit into the life of the first Christians and is celebrated fifty days after Easter because it was supposed to have occurred on the day of the Jewish Pentecost fifty days after Passover. **All Saints' Day** falls on November 1, and is followed by **All Souls' Day**, remembering all Christians who have died throughout history, on November 2. It is a time when families recall deceased members with various memorial observances. Catholics and Protestants observe a Week of Prayer for

75

Christian unity in January. Some Orthodox Christian traditions follow an older calendar so that major religious holidays occur earlier or later than these listings. The Roman Catholic, Anglican (Episcopal), Lutheran, and Orthodox churches follow a calendar of celebrations that is more extensive than some of the other groups. Each denomination observes days that are significant in the history or mission of that tradition.

4

CONVERSION

If a Jew should come to be-
lieve that Christianity is the proper fulfillment of Judaism, that Jesus is the unique son of God who brings
salvation to those who believe in him, then that person
should seriously consider conversion to Christianity.
Conversely, if a Christian should come to believe that
much of Christian theology is mistaken, that God has
chosen the Jews as his "special people" and given them
his unique law as contained in both the written Scriptures and the teachings of the rabbis, to be adhered to
until the end of time, then that person should seriously
consider conversion to Judaism.

Should anyone else consider conversion from one

religion to the other? Possibly. If someone has grown up in one religious environment but has never felt that he or she really belonged there, and has always admired the outlook or way of life of people "on the other side of the fence," then perhaps he should consider becoming part of the other group. If someone has grown up in a harsh and cruel family environment and then encounters people of another religion who take him in as part of their own loving family, then he or she should consider becoming part of the community of this new "family." If someone has grown up devoid of any religious influence and feels that he or she has no spiritual "home" in God's universe, then he should consider adopting another religion as his "home."

Most people, though, will not fall into any of these categories. Most people do not reject either Jewish or Christian theology. (Some people take theology more seriously than others, but very few become convinced that the religious convictions with which they were raised are wrong.) Most people feel at home in the religious community in which they grew up and do not want to reject their family heritage. They do not feel that "the grass is greener on the other side," and conversion is the last thing they would think of.

Many people who would not think of converting will nevertheless seriously consider marriage to someone of another religion. Should the possibility of an interreligious marriage lead them to think about converting to the religion of their marriage partner? What, if anything, is to be gained by such a move? Is marriage alone a sufficient reason to motivate a religious conversion?

In days gone by, many Christians would have answered, Yes, by all means, a Jew should certainly convert to Christianity, for there is no salvation except through faith in Christ. Many Jews, on the other hand, would have said, No, a Christian should not convert to Judaism for the sake of marriage to a Jew, for such a conversion would be based on an unworthy motive. Nowadays, however, the tables have turned. Many Christians would say there is no need for a Jew to convert to Christianity; both religions lead to a knowledge of God and the way of salvation, and a Jew and a Christian who marry each other should preserve their respective religions. Many Jews, on the other hand, particularly those who are not Orthodox, would say that a Christian who wishes to marry a Jew should by all means convert, for the sake of the unity of the family and a harmonious atmosphere in which to bring up children. Jewish parents whose children are contemplating an interreligious marriage are sometimes quick to suggest conversion to Judaism as a way to make it possible for all to "live happily ever after."

Conversion, however, is a viable alternative only for those who are somehow dissatisfied with what they are. If one has theological problems with his or her ancestral religion, or if one is unhappy on a social level with his or her background, then of course conversion should be considered. If one wishes to submerge his or her identity into that of the spouse, then conversion could be a part of that process. But in the age of individualism in which we live, for most people conversion is not a healthy alternative—we are happiest when we accept ourselves as we are. Most Jews and Christians who marry each other will find their happiness not in conversion but in a life enlightened by mutual respect, caring, and sharing, a life in which each religious heritage can enrich the other. The family harmony and unity that conversion is supposed to bring about does not always come into being. If a Christian who converts to Judaism is taught that he or she should no longer commemorate or celebrate Christian holidays in any way, the submerged trauma that can result is often noticeable to spouse and to children. Sometimes, when one parent converts to the religion of the other, children come to look upon that parent's first religion as having been wrested away from them unfairly, and they sympathize and identify with it and perhaps even embrace it during their adolescent years or later. It is possible that interreligious parents can do more for the future happiness of their children by retaining their respective religious identities than they can by converting to the other's religion in the hope that this will produce a unified family. The unity that is produced may prove to be a spurious one.

BECOMING A JEW

When someone who was not born into Judaism decides that he or she wishes to become a Jew, the first task is to find a rabbi willing to supervise the instruction in Jewish principles and preside over the ritual that actually inducts the candidate into the Jewish faith and people. If marriage to a Jew is the motive for seeking conversion to Judaism, an Orthodox rabbi is not supposed to receive the applicant for instruction. The only acceptable motive, from the standpoint of Orthodoxy, is the conviction that God revealed Himself to the

Jewish people through the Torah, both the Hebrew Scriptures and the later teachings of the rabbis, and that these texts and the ideas they promulgate are the ultimate divine truth. Even if the candidate is motivated by this conviction, it is customary for an Orthodox rabbi to urge him to desist from his desire. After all, one does not have to be a Jew, according to Judaism, in order to be righteous in the sight of God and attain salvation. But according to custom, if the applicant returns a third time after having been sent away by the rabbi, then this is a sign of true sincerity, and the rabbi is supposed to receive the applicant for instruction.

In Reform and Reconstructionist Judaism, however, the attitude is quite different. These branches of Judaism regard marriage to a Jew as an eminently desirable motive for conversion to Judaism. Rabbis from these groups would be concerned that at the time of conversion the candidate not harbor any vestigial allegiance to Christian concepts, such as the Trinity or salvation through Christ. But they are willing to accept applicants for instruction in Judaism, leading to the possibility of conversion, even if these applicants have very little knowledge of the religion. A contemplated marriage or an already accomplished marriage to a Jew, or even a desire to become a Jew because "the Jewish way of life" is attractive, is an acceptable reason for seeking conversion, according to most rabbis in these two groups. Reform Judaism has developed an extensive "outreach program" on a national scale, seeking to inform people who might be interested in Judaism, particularly those married to Jews, about the possibility of conversion. Within Conservative Judaism there are two schools of thought. Most Conservative rabbis are probably close to the Reform position, but a number would lean to the Orthodox attitude and prefer that converts not be motivated by anything other than theological conviction about the truth of Judaism.

Instruction leading to conversion includes courses in Jewish history and theology, the Bible and rabbinic texts, the observance of the Sabbath and holidays, the making of a Jewish home, the prayers in the synagogue and, in many instances, the rudiments of reading Hebrew. Instruction might be given by the rabbi on an individual basis or in classes sponsored by several rabbis or synagogues together. Candidates are taught that the first step in becoming a Jew is the acceptance of "the yoke of the kingdom of Heaven"—in other words, the sovereignty of the One God over all that is or will be. The second step is the acceptance of "the yoke of the commandments." According to Orthodox Judaism, the commandments are embodied in the Halacha, both the ethical and ritual requirements contained in the Scriptures, the Talmud, and the later codes of law. Orthodox rabbis in general will not accept the validity of non-Orthodox conversions because, they say, the convert who is instructed by a Conservative, Reform, or Reconstructionist rabbi is not taught that he or she must live by the Halacha. Learning something about Jewish history and philosophy is not enough; there must be an indoctrination in how to live according to Jewish ritual law, including the dietary restrictions and the prohibition of sexual intercourse during the menstrual period. Since the other branches of Judaism do not emphasize these matters, Orthodox rabbis as a rule will not accept their conversions. The other branches, however, accept the validity of Orthodox conversions. Among Conservative rabbis there is a variation in practice. Some accept the validity of Reform conversions while others do not.

Courses of instruction for conversion may last from three months to a year. If at the conclusion of the course the candidate still wishes to become a Jew and is willing to forswear allegiance to any other religious system, the rabbi will make arrangements for the ritual ceremonies that induct one into Judaism. In many cases the rabbi calls on two rabbinic colleagues so that the three together can constitute a "rabbinic court" to examine the candidate about his or her knowledge of Judaism. The next step would be, in the case of a male convert, the ritual circumcision performed by a *mohel,* the expert trained in the Jewish circumcision procedure. In the case of someone who had already been medically circumcised, the *mohel* would draw a symbolic "drop of blood of the covenant" in order to satisfy the ritual requirement. The final step, in the case of both men and women, would be immersion in the ritual bath (*mikveh*). The rabbi arranges for the "court" of three rabbis, or perhaps the rabbi and two laymen, to witness the immersion of the unclothed convert in the pool of water. (In the case of a woman, the group of men stay outside the door for reasons of modesty and depend on the word of a female witness that the convert has immersed herself fully in the ritual bath. If the convert is a man and the rabbi or a witness is a woman, a similar procedure would be followed.) The convert emerges from the water as a new person, bearing a Hebrew name and reborn as the youngest child of Abraham and Sarah.

The ritual in Reform Judaism often is different from what has been described. Reform does not require adult circumcision (even the other branches of Judaism do not require it if it would be medically dangerous), nor does Reform require the immersion in the *mikveh*. Most Reform conversions do not include these rites, though some converts elect to have one or both of them. In the majority of cases the rabbi conducts a conversion ceremony at the synagogue or at home, blessing and welcoming the convert into the fellowship of the Jewish faith and people in the presence of an assembly of family and friends.

CONVERSION TO CHRISTIANITY

Although Christianity began as a movement in Judaism, before the end of its first century it had become a separate religious tradition. Regardless of the overwhelming amount of common ground shared by Christians and Jews, nearly two thousand years of separate histories cannot be overlooked. While it is true that Christianity has utilized conversion as a major instrument of growth, no responsible clergy would encourage a Jew to convert to Christianity simply on the basis of an interfaith marriage. Conversion in Christianity implies a commitment to the basic tenets of the Christian faith, which includes family, parish, worship, and esthetic traditions.

A Jew in an interfaith marriage should consider converting to Christianity only if he or she is moved ultimately by its particular claims about the nature of God and humanity. A Jew does not need to convert in order to participate in much of the life of a Protestant or Catholic church where the spouse is involved. This often occurs in an interfaith marriage where the Christian partner is involved in parish life.

To convert, a Jew should make a thorough inquiry of a particular Christian tradition. Virtually all require a period of preparation. In some cases it may be an informal discussion and study with a clergy person. In others an "inquirer's class" will be offered, accompanied by required readings. Each convert will be asked to affirm one of the classic Christian statements of faith concerning the nature of Christ, and most traditions require an understanding and affirmation of the tri-une nature of God (Trinity). Conversion is completed when the candidate receives the sacrament of Baptism. Among the varieties of Christianity one can find at least as many differing approaches to faith as exist in various Jewish understandings of their tradition and culture.

The love of one partner for the other surely includes honoring the religious tradition of the other, but this is not an adequate basis for conversion to either Judaism or Christianity. Conversion can perhaps "solve" some of the challenges to an interfaith marriage but only if the converted individual enters into a new tradition wholeheartedly and without reservation. Respect for, support of, and, as possible, participation in the religious tradition of one's spouse in many cases is the better way for an interfaith marriage to bridge the differences successfully. Conversion is really an individual step. Though it is often discussed in relation to interfaith marriages, it belongs to another dimension of life.

As indicated elsewhere, certain groups within Protestantism whose primary goals are evangelistic in nature may place considerable pressure on the Jewish spouse to convert to their particular brand of Christianity. In most cases a member of one of these would probably shy away from even dating a Jew. But since it is often true that the particular religious commitment of an individual is among the last things discussed in the romantic relationship, inquiries should be made before finding oneself too deep in a situation from which no easy exit is possible.

The Catholic Church, like most Protestant groups, rejects the idea that anyone should convert because he or she wishes to marry a Catholic. Conversion should be based solely on a deep-seated commitment to Catholicism and its teachings. A Jew who marries a Catholic is encouraged to practice his or her own faith within the context of the marriage.

5

ARRANGING YOUR WEDDING

THE JEWISH WEDDING CEREMONY

Assume that you wish to marry, and one of you is Christian and the other Jewish. Neither of you wishes to convert. You have decided that you would like a Jewish marriage ceremony. What should you do?

At the very outset you should realize that the majority of rabbis will not be willing to officiate at your ceremony. Orthodox and Conservative rabbis are bound by Halacha, Jewish traditional law, so they are unable to marry you even if they wish to do so, since Halacha very clearly prohibits the marriage of a Jew to a non-

Jew. Reform and Reconstructionist rabbis are not bound by Halacha except to the degree that they voluntarily assume it upon themselves. About half of the rabbis in these groups may be willing to marry an interreligious couple. The other half will refuse to do so under any circumstances, believing that it is both contrary to Jewish law and destructive of the Jewish people for such a marriage to take place. They may feel deeply for you and for the difficulties you are experiencing, they may wish they did not have to reject you, but their hands are tied. If you are really bent upon marriage to each other, then you should choose a civil ceremony, they say, or a Unitarian minister, but certainly not a Jewish ceremony, for your marriage is not, in their eyes, a "Jewish marriage." You of course should respect these rabbis and the decision they have made, and realize that you cannot ask them to betray their convictions. Theirs is not the last word, however, for many Reform rabbis may be willing to officiate at your wedding. You have to be patient in your search, though, until you find the right one.

Rabbis who will officiate at the marriage of an interreligious couple have various points of view and philosophies of Judaism. What unites all of them, however, is the conviction that they are called to serve the needs of human beings, not just an abstract body of doctrine. They are also united in feeling that they do more to serve the health and well-being of the Jewish community by their willingness to officiate at interreligious marriages than their colleagues who refuse to do so. The rabbis who are willing to officiate often have individual requirements, such as commitments about the religious education of children or a certain number of hours of premarital counseling. A listing of Reform rabbis who will officiate at interreligious marriages is published periodically by the Rabbinic Center for Research and Counseling, 125 East Dudley Avenue, Westfield, New Jersey 07090. It is an especially helpful list because it details the specific requirements set by the various rabbis. There may be others who are not listed but who are available for wedding services, so it is best to inquire in your own community as to who might be receptive to your needs. Some rabbis who are themselves unwilling may share the names of others who will officiate. You might also contact Christian clergy, who often know of rabbis who will officiate, but perhaps the best source of information is the pool of interreligious couples who have already been married.

A cantor who is willing to officiate at an interreligious wedding is just as suitable as a rabbi. (A cantor is a trained musician who leads the worship services at a larger synagogue. He often is a teacher of religion and may be as well versed in all aspects of Judaism as many rabbis.) The only factor you need to be concerned about, aside from your own personal compatibility with the person you engage for the service, is whether that person is properly licensed to officiate in the locality where your wedding will take place. Some jurisdictions are very particular while others permit any and all clergy to marry within their boundaries. If you are not sure whether a particular rabbi or cantor is licensed to perform marriages in the wedding location, check with the civic officials and inquire about the procedures necessary for him to become properly registered. (If you are having an "ecumenical" ceremony, one involving both Jewish and Christian clergy, only one of the clergy needs to be civilly licensed to officiate—the one who will sign your marriage license and file it with the civil authorities.)

If you are planning a Jewish wedding, one matter that you should be concerned with, in addition to finding a rabbi or cantor who will officiate, is the day on which the ceremony is to take place. In traditional Jewish practice, a wedding is not scheduled on the Sabbath (that is, Friday night or during daylight hours on Saturday) or on major Jewish holidays. Orthodox and Conservative rabbis will not officiate on the Sabbath, nor will most Reform rabbis, although a few will, believing that the reasons not to have a Sabbath afternoon wedding are not compelling. The prohibition of the practice is based on the fact that in ancient times a wedding was primarily a business transaction, the "acquisition" of the bride by the groom. In addition, Sabbath weddings were not approved because the Sabbath, as a day of joy, deserved to be celebrated in its own right while the wedding, as another occasion of joy, deserved its own distinct celebration as well. Rabbis who are willing to perform Sabbath weddings do so because they feel that, first, we no longer regard a wedding as a business transaction and, second, the joy of the wedding enhances the joy of the Sabbath. If you plan to have your wedding on a Saturday afternoon, you will have to restrict yourself to rabbis who are willing to officiate at that time. Even more important than the attitude of the rabbi, however, are the feelings of the Jewish family members who will be involved in the wedding. If they have strong objections to a Sabbath wedding, then it would be best to schedule it when they can celebrate with full heart, such as a Saturday night or a Sunday.

Unlike the matter of when a wedding might be held, the question of where a Jewish ceremony may take place can be answered very simply: anywhere. Jewish ceremonies take place most commonly at the same facility where the reception is held, whether it be a home, a hotel, or a restaurant. Many ceremonies are held outdoors (Orthodox tradition even recommends that the ceremony be outdoors so that the offspring of the marriage might be as numerous as the stars in the sky). While ceremonies may take place in a synagogue, there is no requirement that this be done. Some Orthodox Jews actively disapprove of synagogue weddings. What is unique about the setting of a Jewish wedding is the presence, in many cases, of the *huppa*, the canopy under which the bride and groom stand during the ceremony. The *huppa* may be a cloth draped over poles that are held by four people, or it may be an elaborate free-standing floral production. The *huppa* is emblematic, most anciently, of the bridal chamber; it also recalls the days when all wedding ceremonies took place out of doors and the bride and groom were honored by the protection of a canopy, for they were, for that time at least, "king and queen" like Solomon and his bride in the biblical Song of Songs. Some sort of *huppa* would be required by Orthodox and Conservative rabbis, but optional with Reform rabbis.

In the Jewish wedding tradition, the signing of the religious marriage document, or *ketuba*, takes place prior to the ceremony. The document is prepared by the rabbi and signed by two witnesses. In an interreligious wedding some rabbis give the couple a *ketuba* while others do not. If you are concerned about this, be sure to tell your rabbi or cantor in advance that you would like a *ketuba*.

The wedding procession will most likely include the same attendants as in a Christian ceremony. What is unique about the Jewish wedding procession is the role played by the parents of the bride and groom. Father and mother escort the groom, and both father and mother escort the bride. In most cases the parents remain standing as part of the bridal party during the entire ceremony instead of being seated with the congregation. There is no requirement, however, that this procedure be followed. Very often in an interreligious wedding the parents are seated. If the parents are to stand with the bridal party and the bride is to be escorted by her father alone, then her mother must leave her seat in the front row to stand with the party.

The rabbi or cantor who officiates at your wedding will very likely wish to follow his own style in rendering the liturgy. An outline of a typical wedding service, which includes Hebrew materials as well as English translations of them, is as follows: invocation, some personal remarks directed to the bride and groom, the blessing of the cup of wine representing betrothal (after which the bride and groom drink from the cup), exchange of vows, exchange of rings, the blessing of the cup of wine representing marriage (the "seven benedictions," after which the bride and groom drink from the cup), pronouncement of marriage, closing benediction, breaking of the glass. Some rabbis may be willing to supplement their service with readings selected by the bride and groom or to have the bride and groom compose their own vows. In general, the Jewish wedding ceremony is a warm, embracing one, without any "sexist" language. Its tone is conveyed by the words of the last of the "seven benedictions," praying that there always will be heard "the voice of joy and gladness, the voice of the bridegroom and the voice of the bride, the jubilant voice of bridegrooms from their nuptial celebrations and of youths from their feasts of song. Be praised, Lord our God, for You gladden both the bridegroom and the bride."

The various elements of the Jewish wedding ceremony are all self-explanatory except for the climactic "breaking of the glass." This act, the crushing underfoot by the groom of a well-wrapped glass object, has been explained in many ways over the centuries. It originated during the Middle Ages, a folk custom for good luck (*mazzal tov*). In many cultures throughout the world a loud noise is supposed to drive away evil spirits, and this is the rationale behind this gesture ending the wedding ceremony. A similar act is recounted in the Talmud (Berachot 31a), and it was this example that prompted the adoption of the custom in the Middle Ages. By now it has come to be regarded by many people, both Jews and others, as the most essential, most characteristic, as well as most dramatic aspect of the Jewish wedding, even though it has no spiritual or legal significance. Contrary to what many people think, the glass that is crushed is hardly ever the wineglass from which the bride and groom have taken wine during the ceremony. This glass or metal goblet is very often a family heirloom that will be retained for use on the Sabbath, holidays, and other festive family occasions.

THE CATHOLIC WEDDING

It almost goes without saying that the Catholic Church's requirements for marriage stem from the concern that it is a very serious, holy, and permanent event. It is not only a union of bodies, minds, and hearts but also of souls. The more careful and considerate the preparation, the more those values will last and sustain the relationship.

There is as yet no uniform set of rules for Catholic marriage preparation that applies to the entire U.S. This will have to wait until the Catholic Bishops' Conference decides on the matter. Until then, each couple will have to rely on information received from parish priests who can explain the requirements in each particular diocese. They are generally similar across the country with some few exceptions. It is wise to make arrangements some months in advance.

Several documents will have to be supplied. The Catholic party in an interreligious marriage will need a recent copy of his or her baptismal certificate. One need not take a day off from work to secure it. Since everyone needs one for marriage, you can call or write the church where it is kept and it will be sent promptly. After the wedding, the priest who officiates sends notice to the parish where the record is kept, and the wedding is recorded in the baptism register.

The Catholic also will need a "letter of freedom" from his parish (your parish is where you live now, not where you grew up). This letter testifies that according to their records and knowledge you are not already married and thus are free to be married in the Catholic Church. To secure the letter it is always wise to call ahead. It then can be prepared for your arrival, or the priest will be available to do it on the spot. Some dioceses require additional documentation, for example, affidavits from one or two family members about your freedom to marry in the Church. A non-Catholic also will have to attest that he or she is free to marry in accordance with Catholic standards.

The priest whom you consult will explain the marriage preparation programs. These vary around the country and are called by different names. The most common term is Pre-Cana, referring to Christ's presence at a wedding in Cana of Galilee. These programs seek to help couples prepare spiritually, socially, and emotionally for their new life together. The priest himself will counsel a couple if the available programs do not suit that couple's schedule. The time spent in these counseling programs is considered an essential element before marriage. Exceptions to attendance at such programs are granted only very rarely. Couples who attend a marriage preparation program receive a certificate that must be filed with their other documents.

Sometime before the wedding the priest will interview the couple, who should bring their documents along. This is called the PMI, the "premarital investigation." Along with information about what parish one belongs to, the baptismal information, and whether one is free to marry in the Church, the priest will ask questions about each party's free consent to the marriage and his or her commitment to a permanent relationship. He will also ask about children. If it is to be recognized as valid in the Catholic Church, the marriage cannot exclude the possibility of children. Regardless of age or station in life, the Church believes the sacrament of Marriage must reflect the possibility of God's fruitfulness. The final question is about the willingness and cooperation of the couple to adhere to the values of the Church about procreation. This is the time for the couple to discuss and receive information on a personal basis about what the Church teaches and how to reflect these values in their married life.

The paperwork usually continues after the interview. In the case of an interfaith marriage, the priest will have to file papers with the diocesan authority for what is called a "dispensation." Since the Church has its own legal system, its canon law, the priests are familiar with its requirements. The priest will need special permission to officiate at an interfaith marriage, since the canons allow a priest to officiate only at the weddings of two Catholics unless dispensation is granted. If the non-Catholic party wishes to marry in his or her own tradition, the priest can secure what is called a "dispensation from form," which allows him to assist at the wedding while the ceremony is conducted according to the rituals of the other religion. If the other minister or rabbi is not amenable to the presence of a Catholic priest at the ceremony, Catholics can still be married in these traditions, and the marriages are valid as long as the proper papers are filed with the parish priest. If dispensations are filed, the marriage is considered valid in the Catholic Church. Whether a priest is present at the ceremony is immaterial.

Any Catholic priest knows that he needs delegation to officiate at a marriage if it occurs outside his parish church. The delegation is received from the pastor of the parish in which the wedding is to take place. In such cases priests resemble law enforcement officers; for example, a New York City policeman is still a policeman in New Jersey but cannot function as one in New Jersey without being deputized or receiving jurisdiction. (Beware the "marrying priest" who is careless about the regulations of the Church; your wedding may not be valid in the Church if he acts without such delegation.)

The place where an interfaith marriage ceremony takes place is a matter of special concern for the Catholic Church. In the New York Archdiocese, weddings are permitted, as the canons suggest, in any sacred space such as a chapel, synagogue, or church. Other dioceses may have their own restrictions or regulations about where weddings may take place; for example, the bishop of New York does not allow weddings outdoors under any circumstances. No matter how much the Botanical Garden, World Trade Center roof, Staten Island ferry, or your aunt's yacht may mean in your life, permission will not be granted. You can be married in a catering establishment or hotel or home if the space is suitable for a dignified ceremony. Consult your parish priest regarding these canons and to learn the bishop's discretions that will enhance the solemnity and religious nature of your wedding ceremony. Utah, Wyoming, New York, and Illinois may reflect different sensibilities about the place of a wedding.

Catholic marriages are recorded in the nearest parish church. Should you need a certificate, it will be issued from that church. If the marriage was solemnized in a non-Catholic ceremony, it is recorded in the home parish, and a notice is sent for the records of the chancery (the diocesan office). Certificates of marriage may be obtained from the home parish.

A word should be said about "the promises." Usually at the time of the premarital interview and the collection of the documentation to be filed for your wedding (baptismal certificates, dispensations, and so forth), the priest will deal with two other issues. The forms and formula may vary from diocese to diocese, but essentially the topics are the same. First, inquiry is made to acquire the information that the Catholic party is not abandoning his or her faith through intermarriage. The priest will elicit a verbal response or present a form to be signed to attest to that fact. On the same form or at the same time the Catholic will be asked whether he or she is willing to do all that he can to share his faith through the Baptism and rearing of the children than may come from their union. (In the past, the party who was not a Catholic had to make this promise, but this was changed by the Vatican Council of 1965.)

Catholic ceremonies at which a rabbi or minister has been invited to participate usually do not take place in the context of a Nuptial Mass. Some localities, including the Archdiocese of New York, do not permit a Nuptial Mass for an interfaith marriage. The marriage ceremony will be complete in itself. It has readings, blessings, prayers, music, and other rituals that make the occasion significant. At some weddings the Virgin Mary may enjoy particular favor. The singing of the Ave Maria is popular as a meditation during the ceremony. Sometimes a Catholic bride will place flowers at an altar or shrine devoted to her in the church.

The timing and other details of the wedding should get some consideration. Sunday mornings are usually difficult times for priests, since they have other duties with their congregations. Particular churches may have rules affecting wedding procedure, such as who may or may not play the organ and the types of music permitted (Broadway tunes and popular songs are more suitable for the reception). Photographs and videos may be restricted. (A story is told of a wedding where the video man had an old system that required elaborate extra lighting. Halfway through the ceremony the fuses blew, and he demanded that the ceremony stop and await their replacement. The priest informed him that there was no custodian on weekends and that the wedding would have to continue without video coverage. The priest told the congregation that since the ceremony could not be captured on film, those in attendance would have to make the effort to remember it.) Churches often set up regulations based on experience. For instance, the throwing of rice after a ceremony may seem nice but on church steps it is dangerous and the cause of skyrocketing liability insurance premiums. While things such as rice may be hard to control, couples making arrangements for a wedding should inquire about the regulations they and their party will be expected to follow.

Fees for the use of the church are determined according to particular local custom. Among Catholics, however, there is one invariable rule: The best man should have something in his pocket for the faithful altar boys who assist the priest.

PROTESTANT MARRIAGE RITES

Among mainline Protestant groups an interfaith marriage raises questions, but it is neither forbidden nor looked upon as a betrayal of an individual Christian's tradition. Interfaith wedding ceremonies are often celebrated in Protestant churches. In many cases the minister or priest would want to be assured of the Protestant partner's relationship to the church (not necessarily the particular parish) so that the services provided would be appropriate. Some pastors gladly adapt the liturgy so that both Christian and Jewish traditions are affirmed in the wedding ceremony. An even better solution is for the marriage to be celebrated in an interfaith wedding ceremony with both a rabbi and a minister officiating. Christianity and Judaism both affirm marriage with joy, and each tradition can contribute portions to the celebration that will enrich it. Most mainline Protestant ministers and priests would be pleased to share the celebration with a rabbi. Requirements must be met, but rarely is the interfaith nature of the relationship a stumbling block from the Protestant point of view.

Among Protestant churches a variety of approaches exist. A few churches require an individual to be a member of that denomination, sometimes even the particular parish in which the person is married. Most, however, will participate in the marriage of any person the pastor believes is adequately prepared for and mature enough to enter into a marriage relationship. If the church selected for the wedding is other than the parish and/or denomination of the Protestant spouse-to-be, an early inquiry should be made. Virtually all Protestant clergy will reject a wedding ceremony if the participants have no religious heritage or interest but primarily want a church wedding "because it is such a beautiful place to get married." In most Protestant congregations the decision is in the hands of the individual pastor, although in churches with episcopal polity the bishop must be consulted in certain instances. For these and many other reasons, begin planning as far in advance as possible.

Nearly all Protestant pastors require a period of counseling and evaluation prior to their involvement in wedding ceremonies. In some traditions a defined course of study is offered in connection with counseling. When both a rabbi and a minister are involved in the planning, most pastors would be pleased to work with a congenial rabbi so that the counseling process can avoid duplication. Pastors are primarily motivated to help a couple make the best marriage possible. Even if they have some reservations, they know that people may be married with or without the church's blessing and so they do all they can to support and help couples with their intentions. However, a minister or priest will not hesitate to communicate concerns that may emerge during counseling. A delay in marriage may be recommended, along with more intense counseling. Ministers and priests have the right to refuse to participate if they are convinced the marriage is not in the best interests of both individuals or if the sacred nature of marriage is not affirmed.

Counseling usually includes a brief psychological, sociological, and cultural profile of the individuals. The pastor asks about the religious traditions of the couple, and each party is expected to be informed about the heritage of the other. They are asked to consider the tradition in which they will raise their children. The Jewish member will not be asked to convert, nor will children of the marriage be expected to be nurtured as

Christians (exceptions to this may occur in certain Southern Baptist, Pentecostal, and evangelical traditions). The pastor also asks questions to elicit emotional stability, the ability to show affection, and whether each party can deal effectively with conflict.

Protestant clergy also usually discuss the sexual dimensions of marriage and ascertain the level of awareness of family planning procedures. Birth control is encouraged, and the couple is counseled not to have children unless they are genuinely wanted and the couple is adequately prepared to nurture them. From a Protestant point of view, sexual relationships within marriage may be enjoyed as a part of a loving relationship separate from procreation. The decision to have children is a separate consideration.

Economic factors that may affect the marriage will be questioned and discussed. The pastor does not raise these questions to interfere in the lives of others but so that the two seeking marriage may together consider essential subjects that can make significant differences in their life together.

The pastor will also plan the wedding ceremony with the couple. Should an interfaith ceremony be possible, both the rabbi and the pastor will want to communicate early in the process. The one who leads in the planning process is usually the clergy person of the institution where the wedding is to be celebrated. If the wedding is to be in a church or other religious setting, set the date and time first with the clergy and the institution before making other wedding plans. Many couples face frustration after having already secured a place for the reception only to find that the church's calendar is filled.

Many Protestant churches have developed their own wedding liturgies, and all have many similarities. Protestant pastors will often offer a couple an opportunity to insert brief selections from poetry and literature or other original writing in the service as well as be involved in the selection of Scriptures to be read. Many will ascertain that the vows themselves are ones that both individuals will wholeheartedly affirm. Most pastors rightly insist that anything utilized in a wedding ceremony, including the music, must be appropriate to the occasion and its setting. Otherwise there is no reason for the marriage to be celebrated in a church. Should the couple wish to be married somewhere other than in a church setting, Protestant clergy may celebrate a marriage in any appropriate place.

Most Protestant wedding liturgies are similar to the outline that follows. Almost all can be adapted to an interfaith celebration. The outline is for a large, public wedding ceremony but can be easily adapted for a small, more intimate setting. Sometimes hymns and other responses for all the people gathered are included. All guests at a wedding are considered participants.

1. Pre-nuptial music; while guests arrive, a brief recital is played on an organ or other instruments.

2. Seating of the parents of the groom and the bride.

3. Processional of the wedding party. The bride is sometimes escorted, usually by her father, but this is not necessary.

4. Wedding liturgy:
   Brief statement about the religious nature of marriage

Invocation (prayer)

Charge to the wedding couple

Declarations of consent that each will marry
the other (if the bride is escorted by
her father or other person, she now
joins the groom)

Readings from Scripture and other sources,
which may be followed by a brief homily or other responses

Marriage vows, repeated to each other

Exchange of rings (one or two)

Declaration of Marriage

Prayers or intercessions, often including the
Lord's Prayer

Blessing of the marriage, followed in some
liturgies by the Eucharist

5. Recessional.

In an interfaith ceremony shared by both a minister and a rabbi, portions of the ceremony will be taken
by one or the other. Most clergy who consent to share
in the performance of interfaith weddings will gladly
work out a meaningful ceremony made up of elements
of both traditions. Should a rabbi not be available to
participate with the pastor in the marriage, discuss the
possibility and appropriateness of including selected
Jewish traditions in the wedding ceremony. Few Protestant ministers would perform adequately as cantors
in chanting the Hebrew liturgy, but musical selections,
particular prayers, and Scriptures from Hebrew tradition may be included.

THE ECUMENICAL CEREMONY

An increasing number of interreligious couples are choosing to have an "ecumenical" wedding ceremony in which a rabbi participates along with a priest or minister. These ceremonies in most instances are very inspiring, both for the bridal couple and for the assembled wedding guests. They enable the couple to be blessed in both the Jewish and Christian traditions, and demonstrate the mutual respect that both families have for each other and for the backgrounds from which they come.

Many priests in the Catholic Church and most ministers from mainline Protestant churches are happy to participate in ceremonies of this type. The rabbis who will do so, however, are relatively few in number. If you would like to have this type of ceremony, you probably should be prepared to call a number of rabbis or cantors before finding one who is willing and available to participate. It is worth the effort, though, for the results will likely be most satisfying.

Ecumenical ceremonies can be held in any type of location or edifice, including churches, synagogues, and interfaith chapels. (Some rabbis will not participate in churches, though there are others who will. Priests and ministers have no problem with participating in synagogues.) Occasionally there will be tension between families over the location of the wedding ceremony, with the Jewish family suggesting a "neutral" place and the Christian family preferring a church. (The Jewish family will only rarely wish a synagogue wedding since Jewish tradition does not insist upon the use of a synagogue for any type of wedding ceremony.) In cases where this tension exists, we recommend the following rule of thumb: When the Christian family has had no ongoing connection with a particular parish church, the appropriate place for the ceremony is a neutral spot such as an interfaith chapel or a suitable space at the reception hall. When the Christian family, however, has had a long-standing tie to the parish church in which they would like to hold the wedding ceremony and has celebrated other family events there, there is no reason they should be deprived of the opportunity of celebrating the wedding there as well. An ecumenical ceremony in an edifice that means so much to them can be a beautiful experience, and the Jewish wedding tradition can be fully represented in the liturgy that will be offered by the rabbi who participates. The deeply held feelings of both families can be respected in this way without disrupting family tradition.

The structure and content of the ecumenical service is, of course, in the hands of the two officiants, though suggestions and input from the bride and groom are often welcome. If the Jewish bride or groom wishes that specifically Christian language, such as the mention of Christ or the Trinity, be eliminated or "toned down" in the text of the Christian clergyman, he or she should discuss it with the clergyman. (The rabbi should not be put in the position of "censoring" what the priest or minister will say, any more than they should "censor" what the rabbi will say.) Some priests and ministers may not be willing to modify their usual ritual, but many of them will. The clergy who most often participate in Jewish-Christian marriages are very likely to keep specifically Christian language to a minimum and will not even have to be asked to do so.

Here is an outline of an ecumenical ceremony that has been very favorably received on numerous occasions and in many different settings: introductory remarks by rabbi and priest (or minister), Scripture reading by priest or minister, reception of vows by priest or minister, exchange of rings under the direction of rabbi, blessing of wine ("seven benedictions") by rabbi after which bride and groom drink of the wine, concluding blessings by rabbi and priest (or minister), breaking of the glass.

The Catholic Church as a whole, and most of its priests, are extremely cooperative in making the necessary arrangements for this type of ceremony. From the point of view of the Church, however, the ceremony is either a Catholic one or a non-Catholic one, depending on the type of dispensation that was applied for. If the ceremony is a Catholic one, then the priest must receive the vows. If the ceremony is a non-Catholic one (in this case, Jewish), then the rabbi must receive the vows. The outline of the ecumenical ceremony must therefore be modified to reflect this. (The Church recognizes, of course, the validity of the marriage on the basis of the dispensation that it granted; a non-Catholic ceremony is regarded as the equivalent of a Catholic one in these instances.) The Church also asks that the civil license reflect the type of ceremony that was performed. The clergy person who received the vows should sign the license.

Most Protestant ministers as well as most rabbis are not as particular about these technicalities. They usually decide which one will receive the vows and which one will sign the license; the priest or minister would be expected to sign it if the marriage took place in a church, while the rabbi would sign it if in a synagogue. In other settings the bridal couple might decide which one should sign it.

Art and Carolyn planned to be married in her hometown in the church where she had grown up, though they had met and planned to live in another city. Since Art knew no rabbis in that town, Carolyn's pastor had a receptive rabbi friend who agreed to share in the wedding ceremony with him. In the marriage preparation and planning Carolyn's pastor counseled with the couple, but they also met with the rabbi. In the wedding itself her pastor opened the wedding and led the couple through their vows. The rabbi led them through the exchange of rings and the wine celebration to the close of the service. Both the rabbi and the minister shared in the final blessing. The couple and both families were delighted that each tradition was affirmed.

6

CELEBRATING RELIGIOUS HOLIDAYS AS A FAMILY

"Home for the holidays" is a great American tradition. For many of us our most cherished memories, even in this mobile and wandering age, are of holidays at home with the family. Christians and Jews alike share in this heritage, but because our culture's calendar has many major holidays imprinted with the majority Christian heritage, Jews may find the Christian emphasis at times a bit overwhelming. Within an interfaith marriage, however, you both have something to give and receive to enhance your celebrations of each other's family holidays. You have possibilities denied to those who have only one culture to embrace. You may be breathless at times, but it can be delightful.

Jews and Christians can affirm their own heritages while sharing them with people of another tradition. Celebrate the meaningful dimensions. Respect the others, and enjoy all of it. For example, Americans of all races and backgrounds participate in Chinese New Year celebrations in San Francisco and New York. Those who are not Chinese do not feel it necessary to apologize for commemorating the Chinese festival, nor do they go about rationalizing why they enjoyed the Chinese observance in spite of the fact that it is not "our holiday." In like manner, no Jew should feel that he has to apologize for participating in Christmas, nor should a Christian have misgivings about enjoying a Jewish festival.

From the Christian perspective a large variation exists for celebrating religious holidays. Protestants, because of their early rural settings in America, have strong home traditions. Catholics, whose origins were more urban, share a rich heritage of European ethnic family celebrations. But this is changing. Today many traditions will be found among even nominal Christians. Some holidays are celebrated in ways that scarcely reflect their religious origins, yet even the most secularized holiday traditions often symbolize their Christian sources. Jews and Christians will find that in their spouse's family tradition many special customs may exist around religious celebrations that are not recorded here. Note them; ask about them; enter into them if appropriate. Often, the family will be pleased.

To begin, the weekly observance of the Christian and Jewish Sabbaths establishes the rhythm of both faiths. We then will consider a year of special observances in each tradition that have specific emphases in the home and family.

Since the weekly Sabbath is the major festival of Judaism, if you wish to impart the true flavor of Judaism to your children you should seriously consider introducing into your home the Friday night observance that takes place at the dinner table. Christianity never abrogated the seventh-day Sabbath of Judaism (Saturday is still called *sábado* in Spanish and Italian). What Christianity did in its early years was specify that the observance of the Sabbath was not *required* on the part of a Christian; the commemoration of the day was never forbidden. Sunday is not the exact equivalent of the seventh-day (Saturday) Sabbath in Christian tradition; it is the "Lord's Day," calling to mind the resurrection event of Easter to those who gather for worship on that day. (The churches have, of course, taken over the Sabbath traditions that mandate abstention from work and applied them to Sunday, so for most Christians Sunday observance has effectively replaced the celebration of the biblical seventh-day Sabbath.)

The Friday night observance begins with the lighting and blessing of the candles, at least two of them, by the woman of the house. The words recited are, "We thank You, Lord our God, Ruler of the world, for You have sanctified us by Your commandments; therefore do we kindle the Sabbath light." The man then blesses his wife, quoting chapter 31 of the book of Proverbs, which begins, "A woman of valor, who can find, for her price is far above rubies." He then blesses his children. For boys, the words are, "May God make you like Ephraim and Manasseh," who were the sons of

Joseph. For girls, the blessing is, "May God make you like Sarah and Rebecca, Rachel and Leah." The blessing of the entire family concludes with words well known to many Christians as well as Jews, "The Lord bless you and keep you; the Lord cause His face to shine upon you and be gracious to you; the Lord lift up His face toward you and grant you peace." (In a fully egalitarian family, the mother would naturally wish to participate in the blessing of the children along with the father, and a wife would presumably wish to bless her husband.)

When the dinner is about to begin, the man of the house blesses the wine and the Sabbath day. The words are, "We thank You, Lord our God, Creator of the fruit of the vine. We thank You, Lord our God, for You have sanctified us by Your commandments and given us the holy Sabbath in love and in favor." The bread is then blessed and distributed with the words, "We thank You, Lord our God, Ruler of the world, for You bring forth bread from the earth." At the Sabbath meal the bread is usually a special braided loaf called *halla.*

Alma and Sal have chosen to incorporate the Friday night observance into their family life. They don't do it every week because sometimes one of them is late getting home from work or has an engagement on Friday night away from home. But when both can be home at the normal dinner hour, they look forward to the feeling of serenity and togetherness that the Sabbath ritual can bring. Their children, too, seven and nine years old, enjoy the ceremony and eagerly await the tasting of the wine and the special bread. Sal does not feel that his participation in any way compromises his Catholic loyalty or identity; rather, it enhances it.

Some synagogues, usually Reform, hold their major Sabbath service on Friday night, at 8 P.M. or thereabouts. Other synagogues schedule their major Sabbath service on Saturday morning. Whether you are raising your children as Jews or as Christians, you should plan to attend these services as a family from time to time. In this way you and your children will grow together in an understanding of this portion of their religious heritage.

Sunday is the Christian day of worship, sometimes called the Christian Sabbath. Early Christians moved from Saturday to Sunday because their worship was primarily the recalling of the Easter experience, which they believed occurred on Sunday. While Sunday is the day of worship for nearly all Christians (Seventh-Day Adventists observe Saturday as the Sabbath), few Christians invest Sunday with as much tradition as an observing Jewish family devotes to its Sabbath (the "blue laws" that once closed most businesses on Sundays are fast disappearing). But most Christians think of Sunday as the Lord's Day, a day of rest and worship. For them it has a quality different from other weekend days, although the proscription against work is losing its influence. Sunday dinner "after church" in some areas continues as a special family meal.

Nearly all Protestant churches schedule their major weekly service, about an hour in length, on Sunday morning between nine and noon. Sunday Church School among Protestants is the primary program for the Christian education of children, youth and, in some areas, adults. It is usually scheduled for an hour before or after the service of worship. Families who elect for their children to be nurtured in a Protestant tradition will want to enroll their children in the Sunday Church School of their congregation. Classes usually begin at the nursery school level and continue through high school, sometimes beyond. In addition, the Christian Education programs of Protestant congregations often plan retreats, family-oriented activities, camping experiences, service projects, and other opportunities to enhance the Sunday School and worship life of the congregation.

Catholic churches have Masses throughout Sunday morning and may also offer a late Saturday afternoon or evening Mass that will fulfill one's Mass obligation. Catholic churches offer special classes for children, youth, and adults as well as through their well developed parochial school system. In some Catholic and Protestant traditions individual Christians keep a morning fast until communion has been received at the Sunday service.

Interfaith couples, regardless of which faith they choose for the primary nurture of their children, will find participation as a family in the Sunday worship celebrations of Christians a way to grow in an appreciation of this dimension of their religious heritage. Most of the family life programs planned in Christian congregations can be enjoyed without hesitation by Jews.

The Jewish holidays that punctuate the year and its seasons are all marked by home observances as well as services in the synagogue. The New Year (Rosh Hashana) and Day of Atonement (Yom Kippur) primarily center about the prayers of penitence recited in the synagogue, but at home they are commemorated by families gathering together. The festive dinner on Rosh Hashana evening begins with the blessing of the candles by the woman of the house, the blessing of the wine by the man, and the blessing of the bread. In many homes it is customary to eat a sliced apple dipped in honey or a piece of bread with honey to express the hope for a "sweet year." The Day of Atonement is a fast day, though a family dinner precedes the beginning of the fast.

Attendance at synagogue services on these "High Holy Days" is more widespread than at any other time of the year. Jews ordinarily make arrangements to take time off from work on these days, and many Jewish-owned companies are closed down completely. If you are married to a Jew, you should seriously consider taking off from work on these days, too, so that you can participate in the spirit of family closeness that is often so apparent then. By taking off from work and visiting the synagogue for at least some of the services, you help to dramatize the importance of these days for the Jewish members of your family. This would be particularly significant if your children are being raised as Jews. Of course, if your work is such that you cannot easily get the time off, your family should understand. You do not have the same obligation as a Jew to celebrate these days, and you should not be expected to inconvenience your employer or your fellow workers by insisting on these days off if it would cause them hardship.

Families who are more into religious observance than the average might want to observe the harvest and thanksgiving festival of Tabernacles by building a tabernacle (*sukka*) next to their home. This is great fun for children and for parents too. The *sukka* is a simple temporary shelter in which the family eats its meals, or at least a symbolic portion of a meal, during the first seven days of the holiday. All that is needed is a make-shift structure with three sides (people who are not construction-minded can obtain prefabricated *sukkas*). The roof consists of the branches and twigs of trees or bushes, the leaves still attached. It is essential that the sky be visible through the branches and leaves. Children can be imbued with a closeness to nature and nature's God by helping to set up the *sukka* and eating there with the family during the festival week. Bunches of fruit often are hung with string from the branches above as decoration. Sleeping overnight in the *sukka* was part of the ancient ritual, but the feasibility of doing this will depend on weather conditions where you live.

Close to the Christmas season is Hanukkah, the remembrance of the heroism of the Maccabees. While the holiday was originally a "minor" one, involving only the kindling of candles on the eight nights, it has evolved into one widely observed even by Jews who are not too punctilious about other ritual obligations. The kindling of the lights is still at the center of activity. One light is kindled on the first night, ascending to eight on the last night. The blessings that are recited are these: "We thank You, Lord our God, Ruler of the world, for You have sanctified us by Your command-ments; therefore do we kindle the Hanukkah light. We thank You, Lord our God, Ruler of the world, for You wrought miracles for our ancestors in days of old at this season." On the first night the following benediction is added: "We thank You, Lord our God, Ruler of the world, for You have kept us in life, and sustained us, and brought us to this season." The Hanukkah candelabrum (menorah) has nine branches—one being the server, the one used to light the others. After the candles have been lit, there are quite a number of Hanukkah songs that might be sung, some old and some fairly new, many of them written for children.

While it has not been customary to celebrate Hanukkah with an elaborate family feast, the Jews of Central and Eastern Europe brought over the custom of eating potato pancakes (*latkes*). These give a warm and filling feeling to those who eat them on cold, wintry nights, and many Jews do not feel the holiday has been adequately observed unless they are able to enjoy their quota of *latkes*. Also from Eastern Europe is the custom of playing *dreidel* on the nights of Hanukkah. The dreidel is a spinning top embossed with four Hebrew letters. The letters also serve as numbers, and there can be quite a lot of friendly competition to see who will amass the highest score as the tops whir across the table or floor.

The specifically American innovation in the observance of Hanukkah is its promotion as a major gift-giving time. In Europe children were sometimes given a few coins as a holiday treat, but on this side of the Atlantic larger and more colorful gifts are in order, complete with distinctive wrappings. Some parents give their children gifts on all eight nights of the holiday. Others feel that this runs the risk of making children too materialistic and demanding, and they restrict themselves to one gift per child for the entire holiday. If you want to observe Hanukkah as a time when you give gifts to your children, you will have to decide which approach you prefer. Of course, another consideration is that eight small gifts might be preferable to one expensive gift. This is an issue that only a high-level meeting of minds between parents can resolve. As might be expected, the celebration of Hanukkah, with its ritual, games, and gifts, is widespread among interreligious families.

> Frank and Cheryl have two children, a boy of seven and a girl of five. Cheryl takes it upon herself to light the candles each night as Frank and the children join in reciting the blessings. Frank, who is a Protestant from New England, has a fine voice and plays the guitar, so he leads a song after the candle lighting. On at least one night of the holiday they have potato pancakes. Frank and Cheryl have chosen to give their gifts to the children on the first night of the holiday unless that night coincides with Christmas. Since they give their children Christmas gifts, they want them to enjoy their Hanukkah presents as a separate experience. In years when the two holidays coincide, their children get their Hanukkah gifts on the eighth night.

Christmas, the celebration of the birth of Christ, can be overwhelming. Even though their clergy sometimes chide them for their excesses, most Christians prefer it that way. Our culture is thoroughly saturated with Christmas traditions. It may be helpful to understand why the traditions grew up, what they mean, and how a Jew may participate without either "becoming" Christian or "relinquishing" essential Jewishness.

Family gatherings around the lighted Christmas tree, gift-giving, much too much to eat and probably to drink, even the cherished ornaments for the tree and home may appear to have little to do with a child's birth nearly two thousand years ago in remote Bethlehem. But the traditions of the love of God and family, of caring for neighbors, and of a winter's celebration of new birth are dimensions of many religious holidays. Historically, many of the customs surrounding Christmas were an adaptation of the Roman feast of Saturnalia (because nobody has a accurate record of when Jesus was actually born). Decorating with greenery and flowers, exchanging gifts, and feasting came into the Christmas festivity from Roman Saturnalia traditions. Dating Christmas on December 25 was adapted from another Roman celebration, the Feast of the Unconquered Sun, commemorating the winter solstice when the days began to lengthen. The Church adapted its life to the culture, and it was an easy transition from the rebirth of the unconquered sun to the birth of the "light of the world" and the "'sun of righteousness." Other Christmas traditions, such as the Yule log, mistletoe, holly, ivy, bay leaves, and the decorated tree, were adaptations of various ethnic and tribal traditions. When the ancestors of modern Europeans were converted to Christianity, they brought their old customs into their new faith and culture. The almost universal practice of carol-singing began in medieval times.

All of the wonderful customs surrounding Christmas are, for Christians, experiences that enhance their affirmation that God's love was expressed in a unique and powerful way in the birth of Christ. Often a beautiful crèche (miniature Nativity scene) will be placed in the same special place in the home every year.

The development of Christmas into a family festival owes much to the writings of Charles Dickens, who influenced traditions both in England and in America. To him Christmas in the home within the family circle symbolized human goodwill. In his books, particularly *Pickwick Papers* and *A Christmas Carol,* he successfully popularized his point of view.

Gift-giving is central to Christmas celebrations. Children are surfeited with gifts from even remote relatives. Parents and grandparents all get into the act, and even an anonymous Santa Claus brings gifts. Everyone becomes a child at Christmas, so gifts abound for all. Small gifts may be relegated to the Christmas stocking, often not a sock but a large boot-shaped cloth container hung prominently on the mantel, one for every member of the family. Most gifts, however, are placed under the family Christmas tree and are opened at family gatherings either on Christmas eve or on Christmas morning. The tradition reflects the Christian affirmation that the birth of Christ was God's great gift of love to humanity, and gift-giving is a way of saying to family and friends that they are loved and cared for. The meaning of the gift is imbued with the personal feelings of the giver, and the recipient accepts it with this knowledge.

Families are expected to be together at Christmas. Christianity doesn't require it; tradition does. The decision about which home to go to often becomes competitive or disruptive. Grandparents want their extended families around them and either invite everyone to their home or wait expectantly for one of their children to host the gathering. Some families have two gatherings: one in one home on Christmas eve, the other at another home on Christmas day. Parents of small children should keep in mind just how exhausting this can be for little people. Such extended family gatherings can be delightful or destructive. Careful planning and open communication are essential. No rule can cover every situation, but in an interfaith marriage it is most important that the Christian partner help the other to understand what is happening and help him or her through the first few experiences. The family Christmas celebration is an event where tradition reigns.

Christmas day often climaxes in a large feast. Christmas dinner centers around turkey, goose, roast beef, or occasionally ham. A Christian spouse should inform family hosts if Jewish guests keep dietary traditions. Many homemade condiments and special dishes may accompany the feast. Traditional pies, fruit cakes, and other desserts abound. In some families everyone is expected to prepare and bring a special food contribution. Again the Christian in the marriage should anticipate expectations. Few experiences are more embarrassing to a young spouse than to learn all too late that everyone else made a contribution that she or he knew nothing about. Christmas dinner begins with a prayer of thanksgiving and blessing (grace; some Christians begin every meal with this prayer). At one time it was given by the head of the family, but today it may be spoken by anyone present. The content of the prayer may be extemporaneous or follow a particular church's liturgical tradition. A typical prayer before a major Christian feast would begin with thanksgiving for the mighty acts of God being celebrated at this meal, followed by a prayer of gratitude for family and food, and concluding with a supplication that those present not forget the needs of others.

During the season preceding Christmas, churches have numerous special services, and many families keep a tradition of going together to church. These services tend to emphasize music, including carol-singing, and many traditions include Communion and a sermon. Many churches have programs especially planned for families with young children. These services are often quite lovely, with the rich and beautiful heritage of Christmas music. Churches and their services provide a reminder to everyone that gift-giving and sharing reach beyond family and friends. Many opportunities are provided to make available help and hope to those with special unfulfilled needs. Attending these services with your family will support and affirm the Christian spouse's heritage and traditions. While they can be scheduled at various times, congregations usually celebrate their major Christmas liturgies on Christmas eve.

Many Christians keep a season of preparation called Advent, the four weeks of penitence leading up to Christmas. An increasing number of Christian families, especially with small children, follow the Advent wreath tradition. The Advent wreath is a circle of evergreens holding four candles, and it is often placed on the family dining table. One candle is lighted on each of the four Sundays before Christmas. Prayers and scriptures are often read. Another tradition, especially in families with children, is the Advent calendar, a colorful calendar made up of windows to be opened on each of the days before Christmas. Families count the days to Christmas with increasing excitement and anticipation.

Art, a Jew, and Carolyn, a Protestant, have been married five years. Art joins with Carolyn in her Christmas celebration. Early in their marriage they agreed to participate to the extent each could in the other's family religious traditions. Art has found that he can join with Carolyn and her family at the Christmas eve service in their church, and enjoy the music and the expressions of love and family life without betraying his Jewish heritage. While many Christmas customs relate symbolically to the birth of Christ, they also can be celebrated as festivals of family togetherness and joy. Art participates in decorating the house, tree-trimming, gift-giving, and many other Christmas traditions. Since Art loves Carolyn, he finds his love enhanced as he shares in some of the customs that she cherishes. In this spirit Art and Carolyn enter enthusiastically into each other's special holidays and family gatherings.

The great spring festival of Judaism is Passover, the remembrance of the exodus from Egypt in the days of Moses. The home commemoration of the holiday is the Seder on the first two nights. This is the time when families come together, sometimes traveling across the country to unite for only a few short hours. The Seder is a very important event in the lives of many interreligious families. What you have to remember, whether you are Jewish or Christian, is that the preparation of an acceptable Seder is *not* an insurmountable task. It is a challenge, but one that can be met by anyone who enjoys setting a formal festive table. (In

Orthodox Judaism all dishes and utensils have to be changed for Passover since they might be contaminated by leaven, but since most interreligious families are not likely to be that meticulous about this aspect of the Jewish dietary regulations, we assume that you in your home will not feel the need to do this.)

Most editions of the Haggadah ("narration"), the book that contains the service to be recited at the Seder, include instructions about how to set the Seder table. In the center should be the Seder plate, which contains the ceremonial symbols of the feast: a roasted bone (representing the Paschal Lamb sacrificed in ancient times), a roasted egg (standing for the other festival sacrifice offered in the ancient Temple), a piece of horseradish or other bitter herb, a portion of *haroset* (a paste made of chopped apples, nuts, cinnamon, and wine, reminiscent of the mortar made by the slaves in Egypt), and a sprig of parsley or lettuce. Near the Seder plate there should be three pieces of matza (unleavened bread) under a cover. These three represent the bread that is eaten every day, the extra portion that is eaten on holidays, and the "bread of affliction" peculiar to Passover, which will be broken later on in the ritual. Also near the Seder plate is a cup filled to the brim with wine. This cup is not to be drunk since it is the "cup of Elijah," symbolic of the redemption that is yet to come in the future.

Each guest should have most of these items at his or her place as well: horseradish, *haroset,* parsley, matza, and wine. The Haggadah will give the details of the ritual along with the blessings to be recited at each step, but the general pattern is as follows: the woman of the house blesses the candles, the man blesses the wine, and all present drink of it; the parsley is dipped in salt water and eaten; the middle piece of the matza that is under the cover is broken and half of it hidden; the youngest child present (or the youngest who knows how to read) asks the "four questions" (the text that begins, "Why is this night different from all other nights?"); the story of Israel's slavery and exodus from bondage is recounted in answer to these questions; some psalms of thanksgiving are recited or sung; a second cup of wine is drunk by all present; matza is blessed and eaten; the horseradish is blessed and mingled with *haroset* and eaten; some horseradish mingled with *haroset* is placed on matza and eaten; and the meal is served. There are no set requirements as to what the meal must include, but a meat is ordinarily the main dish (except for vegetarians). Other foods often served as part of the meal are hard-boiled eggs and gefilte fish.

During the meal the children search for the broken piece of matza that has been hidden. The one who finds it "holds it for ransom." After he or she gets a prize or reward, this piece of matza is broken and distributed to all the guests and eaten. It is supposed to be the last solid food taken at the meal. The grace after the meal is recited or sung, the third cup of wine is drunk, the final psalms of thanksgiving are recited, the fourth cup of wine is drunk, and the evening concludes with the set of madrigals and songs at the end of the Haggadah.

If you are cooking and setting the table for the Seder, a few items of additional advice might be helpful: First, do not put any leavened or ordinary bread on the table. The matza takes the place of bread for the Seder and, for those who observe the traditions of the holiday, it replaces bread until the holiday is over a week later. Second, do not put butter on the table. While matza may be eaten with butter during the rest of the week, it should be eaten plain at the Seder. Third, even if you do not observe the traditional rules about allowable or kosher meats during the rest of the year, do not serve "forbidden" foods (such as shellfish and pork) at the Seder. Fourth, do not serve cocktails since liquor is made from fermented or leavened grain, which is prohibited during the holiday.

The Seder is a time when families come together, but it is also a time when those who are alone or have nowhere else to go are invited as well. The spirit in most households is not one of solemnity but of joy. Those present should not talk during the readings from the Haggadah, but in between paragraphs it is perfectly acceptable to interrupt with a question or a comment, even if it borders on the ridiculous. It is expected that young children will make noise, and they should not be punished for it. Children are given prominence at the Seder at the reading of the "four questions" and during the search for the hidden matza. In many households the readings from the Haggadah are divided among all the guests present. If you are not Jewish, do not be afraid that your reading will not measure up to that of the others at the table.

In Richard and Lori's home, the Seder is the highlight of the year. Lori is Catholic, but she has mastered the art of preparing the food and the table for the evening. They always invite both his parents and her parents, as well as two or three other couples with their children. Some are Jewish, others are not. Richard and Lori's son is seven and, with help, he is able to make his way through the reading of the four questions in English. When he is older he will read them in Hebrew. There is always a lot of noise and laughter at the table, though it does not detract from the dignity of the service. The Seder celebrates the liberation of Israel from bondage and its journey to freedom, and those who come to Richard and Lori's Seder are able to depart each year with an appreciation of what freedom means and the kind of spirit that reigns when it is present.

The major spring Christian holiday, Easter, is perhaps more Church- than family-centered, but it, too, is celebrated in the home. More Christians go to church on Easter Sunday than on any other day of the year. Often non-Christians are confused about just when Easter is celebrated. Easter's date was not really settled in the Church until the fourth century. The problem centered about the concern to keep the celebration related to its two historical connections. Because Jesus' Last Supper was thought to be a Passover meal, Easter should logically follow the Passover holiday. And with the belief that the Resurrection occurred on a Sunday, this became the Christian "Lord's Day." In A.D. 325 it was finally decreed that Easter would be determined by the first full moon that occurs on or after the spring equinox (March 21). The earliest date for Easter Sunday is March 22, and the latest is April 25.

Once again a feast for the extended family is often celebrated, although distant family members don't make a pilgrimage home for Easter as often as at Christmas. Spring lamb or ham is often served at a family Easter dinner that usually begins with a blessing prayer similar to the one described for the Christmas feast. If Easter occurs during the Jewish Passover season, matza should be served for Jewish guests in addition to the usual bread. Jews traditionally do not eat leavened bread during Passover.

Decorated Easter eggs are an ancient tradition, and children often engage in an egg hunt or roll on the newly sprouted spring grass. The egg symbolizes new life out of old, but it is as much a symbol of spring as of Easter and the Resurrection. The color at Eastertime in the church is white, and frequently lilies are given as an Easter gift or as a memorial to a deceased family member.

A Jewish spouse will sometimes be surprised when a Christian insists that the children have new clothes for Easter. This tradition is not as firm as it once was, but in America, Christian families have long decked everyone out in new Easter "finery." It stems from the ancient association of Easter with Baptism and the new clothes worn by those who entered the faith at this season.

Lent, the season of preparation for Easter, is widely and solemnly observed. For forty days, beginning on Ash Wednesday and excluding Sundays, the Christian penitent prepares for Easter, often by voluntarily assuming a special discipline. This may include periods of meditation, Bible study, special acts of service, or fasting. Lent is an individual discipline and may be an important part of the spiritual life of the Christian spouse, and a significant portion of it may be observed at home.

Holy Week, the final week before Easter, is a time of contrast. It begins with a celebration of Jesus' triumphal entry into Jerusalem. Many churches begin their services with palm processionals and give each worshiper a palm branch or cross. On Thursday evening Jesus celebrated the Last Supper with his disciples, and this became the source of the Eucharist (communion) celebration. On Friday, the day of crucifixion, churches have special liturgies. This is the most somber day of the Christian calendar, and many Christians devote at least part of the day to prayer and fasting. Other special services observed in some Christian traditions include an Easter vigil at night on the eve of Easter (Saturday) and an Easter sunrise service. Family participation in these services is a strong tradition in many churches.

Holy Week services often include the Gospel narratives of the passion story. A Jew attending some of these services may hear Christian scriptures that sometimes have been interpreted as holding the Jews responsible for the crucifixion of Jesus. Their point was that Jesus was rejected by the people of his time. The interpretation in the Church today is that people of conscience who challenge the establishment and the status quo are often rejected by their own communities in almost every tradition. Such individuals become milestones in human history, from the prophet Jeremiah to the Reverend Martin Luther King, Jr. The purpose of these readings is not to cast blame on any group but to encourage the worshiper in self-evaluation with regard to his or her own betrayal of the love and compassion that Jesus stood for in the world. The betrayal of Jesus is considered by Christians to be a universal human failure, and the Christian Church today decries the singling out of Jews as responsible for his death as anti-Semitism of the worst kind.

Celebration of Christian holidays among families is quite varied. Communication between husband and wife about these traditions well ahead of the date can help to ease anxieties and relieve possible tensions. If the two of you agree on a common approach, it creates a very positive means of responding to conflicting requests from your extended family. A person may be unaware of just how important these family celebrations are to a spouse whose traditions are not the same. It is in these traditions that families often cement their relationships. They often cost little and are enjoyable, and the establishment of family ties will be worth the investment. Regardless of which tradition you choose for the rearing of your children, the involvement of your family in the dual family heritage will enrich their lives and give them a sense of respect and gratitude for each parent's culture and faith. You have the right to expect your spouse's family to respect your own heritage, as you respect theirs.

When Asher and Dorothy planned to be married, the question of an interfaith marriage meant little to Asher. He was born into a Jewish family but had seldom, if ever, practiced any of his Jewish religious traditions. Since Dorothy was a committed Christian, they were married in a Christian church setting and, because of Dorothy's interest, decided early on that their two daughters would be raised in that faith. However, Dorothy wanted their children to know about and appreciate their father's heritage. She asked Asher about the meaning of the great Jewish holidays and how they could be celebrated in the family. Asher appreciated his wife's concern but had to confess that he knew little about the traditions.

Through his wife's encouragement Asher studied and learned about his tradition and became a more active participant in Judaism. Because the family kept and celebrated the Jewish as well as Christian festivals, their children grew closer to their father and came to revere and respect his culture and heritage.

Later on, Asher confided in a friend that had he not married an active Christian, his children probably would have been reared with no religious training at all, and that because of the interest of his wife he became a far better Jew than he had ever been before.

7

HOW SHOULD
WE RAISE
OUR CHILDREN?

"What are you going to do about your children?" These are the words that parents, sometimes with a nervous edge to their voices, often address to their child upon learning that he or she plans to marry someone of another religion. Sometimes the question comes from other relatives or even casual acquaintances. Children may not even be in the picture for a number of years, but still people want to know: What are you going to do about your children? Interreligious couples are often tempted to answer, and sometimes actually do, "It's none of your business." But still the question persists in their own minds. Should the children be raised with no religion or with both? Should they be raised as Christians or as Jews? Should the choice be left to the children themselves or to the parents? Should they be raised in a third faith so that neither the Jewish nor the Christian parent feels "offended"? Should boys be raised in one faith and girls in another? Or perhaps a kind of lottery should be played: If the first child is a girl, all children will be raised as Christians (or Jews); if the first child is a boy, all children will be raised as Jews (or Christians).

We cannot supply you with a magic answer to this dilemma, but we hope that we can give you some helpful strategies for dealing with it. Thousands of interreligious families are raising children to be healthy, happy, and fulfilled individuals. You should not fear that the challenge will be too difficult for you. People of goodwill and respect for each other can and do work together in an atmosphere of love, caring, and sharing to give their children a spiritual direction.

The first point we would like to emphasize is that neither Christianity nor Judaism can be the "wrong" choice for your child. The choice of "no religion" is wrong, in our judgment, because it will shortchange your child in the future. If you believe that there is a God who is involved with human life, then you would not want your child to be denied the opportunity of the relationship with Him that religion provides. On a social level, most people are involved with a religion to some degree, and if your child has to identify himself or herself as a person of "no religion," the child quite likely will feel deprived. The choice of one religion for boys and another for girls is also wrong, in our judgment, because it may sow an unnecessary confusion where confusion need not exist. A Jew who can marry

133

a Christian should not, by any logic, think that Christianity is "wrong" for his or her children. Conversely, a Christian who can marry a Jew should not think that Judaism is "wrong" for his or her children. Both are roads to a knowledge of God and to a sanctification of life.

Another point we would like to emphasize is that no parent whose children are being raised in the religion of the other parent should feel "offended" or "left out." Just as fathers can be close to daughters, and mothers to sons, so can Christian parents be as emotionally tied as Jewish parents to their children who are being raised as Jews, and vice versa. Children develop various interests and talents over the years that may or may not be shared with parents. Children who are athletes or musicians may have parents who don't know the difference between a bat and a ball or between a trombone and a tuba, but that should not come between the parent-child relationship. What is important is the interest and concern the parents take in their children's progress and the pride they have when their children accomplish goals they have set for themselves. This is as true in religious development as in other fields. Jewish parents can take pride in the religious growth of their Christian children, and Christian parents can rejoice in the studies and accomplishments of their Jewish children with no sense of being "unfaithful" to their own religious tradition.

As we pointed out in the chapter about wedding arrangements, the Catholic Church requires the Catholic party in an interreligious marriage to undertake, to the best of his or her ability, to raise children as Catholics. There is nothing similar within the Protestant tradition, though some individual churches and ministers attempt to impose their own requirements. Many rabbis, too, specify before they will officiate at an interreligious marriage that they must receive a promise the children born of the marriage will be raised as Jews. Many people recognize, however, that some of these promises may not be kept, and the wording of the statement required by the Catholic Church implicitly accepts this. If circumstances prevent the Catholic party from living up to the promise, then he or she is free of that obligation. The Church does not wish to see marriages broken up over this issue, and it recognizes that the spiritual welfare of the family unit, including the children born and yet to come, is paramount. When parents seek to decide the issue of religion for their children, they should survey the possibilities from a similar perspective: What choice will best serve the welfare of the family unit? What choice will best enable the children to develop as autonomous and happy persons, loving God and their fellow human beings, knowing something of the good, the true, and the beautiful, and enriching society by their gifts? Your own unique family situation will determine which religious choice is preferable for your children. There is no easy solution, but neither Christianity nor Judaism would be "wrong."

WHEN A CHILD IS BORN

When a child is born, what rituals should you arrange to welcome him or her into your family? Ideally, father and mother should have decided this before their wedding, but not everyone is able to make this decision in the midst of all the excitement and party-going that precedes a typical marriage. Some couples do not discuss this question until pregnancy is upon them, and some postpone it until their baby has been born. In a Jewish-Christian family the alternatives are as follows: Do nothing. Have a Christian Baptism. Have a Jewish ceremony of blessing and naming. Arrange a combination of Christian and Jewish rites. We do not recommend the first alternative, to do nothing, because it indicates that religion is of little or no importance in the life of the family. The second and third alternatives are acceptable, of course, if the religion in which the child will be raised has been agreed upon in advance and if the grandparents on both sides are reconciled to this decision.

The fourth alternative, a combination of Christian and Jewish rites to welcome the child into his or her family, is the one that Fred and Dawn chose for each of their two sons. Jewish and Italian relatives filled their home. The priest and the rabbi came, and each blessed the child according to his own traditions, and then everyone repaired to a magnificent feast of both Italian and Jewish delicacies prepared by the grandparents on both sides. In this extended family, where everyone not only tolerates but has a positive affection for one another, the birth of each child created an occasion when all could come together to rejoice and give thanks for the blessing they had received. The priest and the rabbi had a major problem, though: Each side was anxious that both clergymen eat to his fullest what they had cooked and baked. As a result, the clergymen went away unable to eat anything more for at least a week!

The combination of Christian and Jewish ceremonies is what we recommend for those situations in which a definite decision has not yet been made. This gives both sets of grandparents an opportunity to rejoice, and it enables the parents to put off the decision for a few years. The combination of ceremonies could involve the baptizing or blessing by a minister or priest, along with the Jewish prayers naming and blessing the child by a rabbi (or other Jewish functionary, since there is no requirement in any form of Judaism that a rabbi must officiate at any religious ceremony). There are not too many rabbis or priests who will consent to participate in this kind of arrangement, though, so it might be easier to arrange for each ceremony to be conducted separately. While Baptism is the first of the Christian sacraments, it would not preclude the child's being given a Jewish religious upbringing later in life if that is what his or her parents decide to do. Likewise, the Jewish blessing would not preclude a Christian education in later years. When a child is born to a family, it comes as a blessing to its parents, grandparents, and all who love it, and it is meet and fitting that both sides of the family have the opportunity to rejoice through language and rites that are meaningful and significant to them. In Chapter 9 we discuss in greater detail the Christian and Jewish ceremonies that follow upon the birth of a child.

WHY SHOULD WE CHOOSE?

Ideally, as we said, decisions about a child's religious identity should be made before marriage. But we do not live in an ideal world, and often this is not done. Frequently a decision is made by the time a child is born, but again, this is not always the case. You might quite logically ask, as many have done and will continue to do, "Is it really necessary to choose a religion for our children? Why not expose them to both Christianity and Judaism, and maybe other religions too, and let them choose later on in life?" If religion is not that important to you, then it is not necessary for you to choose one for your children. They presumably will participate at the Christmas party at one grandmother's house and at the Passover Seder at the other grandmother's, so one conceivably could say that they have been exposed to both traditions and are in a position to choose. If this is all the exposure they have to religion, however, they will be in no position to make an intelligent choice except perhaps in a gastronomic sense. Unfortunately, though, all too many interreligious couples think that this is all that is necessary for the religious development of their children. They miss out on the deeper aspects of faith, the philosophy, the history, the examples provided by the saints and martyrs, and are restricted to an understanding of religion as "fun and games" around the dinner table. The fun and the games are important, and the sense of God's presence at a community meal is older than the Bible itself, but these children will be deprived of a great deal that faith has to offer. Though it is difficult for rabbis, priests, and ministers to admit it, these children can still grow up to be happy and good people; the love shown to them by parents is more important to their development than anything they can learn from schools, churches, and synagogues. We feel strongly, though, that children should receive a religious upbringing, not because they will grow up immoral or neurotic without it but because it will expand their horizons in a spiritual direction and will lead them to apprehend a world of beauty and inspiration they would otherwise never know.

Some parents want their children to grow up with a knowledge of God and an appreciation of spiritual truths but do not feel that institutional religion is necessary to accomplish these goals. If such parents are committed to this point of view and take the time to find various religious books to read and discuss with their children, they can expand their own spiritual and intellectual horizons at the same time that they accomplish what they seek for their children. Bible stories can be read at home, and religious holidays can be celebrated at home. Children brought up in this way can grow up to be loving, moral, and happy, believing in a merciful and generous God. We feel, though, that these children will lack an exposure to the community aspect that all religions possess. Faith involves not only a relationship with God, but it also requires a religious community beyond the bounds of the family. One cannot be a Jew in isolation; you need to feel that you are part of the people of Israel. Likewise, a Christian must feel a part of the Church, the "people of God" who exist throughout the world. That is why we advocate that children in an interreligious family be given the opportunity to grow up in either a church or a synagogue setting. They should learn about both parents'

religions but be given a chance to belong to and participate in one of them during their formative years.

Why restrict interreligious children in this way?
Why not send them to both a church and a synagogue
instead of only one? The answer is that it is too confusing for a child to attend both church and synagogue,
or the educational programs they offer, on a regular
basis. There is only so much time in a week, and young
children are not ready to handle the contradictory theologies they might be exposed to if they attend both
church and synagogue. Occasional visits with one or
both parents to both houses of worship—by all means
yes. But let your children receive their primary religious training in one or the other. In this way they can
develop an emotional tie to one of the great religious
traditions while appreciating the other that is part of
their background. This emotional tie will bind them to
a faith that can inspire and comfort them later in life.

HOW CAN WE DECIDE?

You might ask, "If it is better to choose one of our
religious traditions in which to raise our children, how
can we make the choice?" For some people the answer
is simple. If one parent is more actively involved with
or emotionally attached to a religion, that can determine the choice of religion for the children. In a home
where two religions are present, children should learn
about both of them and participate in the holidays of
both traditions, but they should follow the religion of
the parent who is more actively involved in religious
life. This is an approach that logical people should

take, though we recognize that sometimes even the most intelligent and educated of people are not logical when dealing with such an emotional issue. Your emotion, however, should be directed toward the welfare of your child and the welfare of your family unit as a whole.

While the decision about religion for children is rarely a simple one, families where one tradition is clearly dominant have an easier time making a choice. But what about families in which both parents are equally attached to the religious traditions in which they grew up? The largest percentage of interreligious families falls into this group. These people are proud of their faith, attend church or synagogue on the major holy days, and celebrate their faith's religious occasions. They feel that it is important to give their children a firm foundation in a religious tradition but are not sure how to choose one without hurting one set of grandparents or perhaps feeling that they have forsaken the faith for which some of their ancestors may have died. For these intermarried parents, the choice of a religion for their children is difficult indeed. In some cases their emotional turmoil expresses itself not so much in a demand that their children be raised in their own faith but in an insistence that their children *not* be raised in the religion of their spouse. This may not appear to be a sensible or logical reaction, but when caught in an emotional dilemma, sense and logic do not always dictate the response.

Now we have to spend some time talking about guilt. Both Judaism and Christianity are unsurpassed in their ability to induce feelings of guilt. If you fear that you will hurt one set of grandparents by your

141

religious decision, you can go to them and point out that their grandchildren will still be exposed, both at home and through their influence, to the religious traditions that they hold dear. You should not feel guilty about your choice because your primary responsibility is to your children and their welfare. As to the feeling that you may have desecrated the memory of your ancestors who died for their faith, this is more likely to be found among Jews than among Christians. If you felt this way strongly before you were married, then you never should have married someone who was not a Jew. But if they rise to consciousness only after your children are at hand, you should ask yourself how you can best honor the memory and the sacrifices of the martyrs of the past. It is by rearing children who would do them honor by the ethical tone of their lives. Here, too, it is the welfare of your children that must be paramount.

Parents who insist that their children not be raised in the religion of the other parent do so because they regard their children essentially as extensions of themselves. (The other parent was only incidental in the procreative process.) When it is the man who is afflicted with this feeling, it is often the reflection of an Old World culture in which the man, as head of the house, makes all the major decisions. For a child to be raised in the religion of his mother would be an affront to the "manhood" of his father. This is an attitude that perhaps was defensible years ago but has only limited usefulness in today's world.

When Irma and Steve went to the rabbi to discuss their forthcoming marriage, it was Irma who declared very firmly that she would "never allow her child to be raised Catholic." She didn't know why she felt that way; she just did. She really didn't care that her children be Jewish, only that they not be Catholic. Since Steve was not that committed a Catholic, Irma might be able to get her way without too much family turmoil. As the years go on, perhaps Irma will develop more of a positive interest in Judaism. At least it is to be hoped that she will develop less of a negative response to Catholicism.

From a strictly logical perspective, one might ask a parent, "If you could fall in love with someone of another religion, why couldn't your children share the religion of the person you love?" From this point of view, children can be seen not as extensions of the self but rather as the fruit of the love that the parents share for each other. It is this approach, we think, that should guide parents when they seek to decide the vexing question of which religion they should choose for their children. Ego involvement should be kept to a minimum. The emphasis must be on the love that is shared between father and mother, and the love they extend to their children.

THE RELIGIOUS COMMUNITY

If Judaism is the religion of choice for your children, then you should be aware that in Orthodox and Conservative synagogues only someone born of a Jewish mother is considered Jewish by birth. Many of these synagogues will refuse to accept into their educational programs children whose mothers are not Jewish. Conversion to Judaism is possible for these children, as it is for anyone else, but only someone who is thirteen years of age or older is eligible to convert since it must be an "adult" decision. If a woman who is not Jewish converts to Judaism before her children are born, both she and her children are considered Jewish by Orthodox and Conservative standards. If she converted after they were born, however, they retain a non-Jewish status until they seek conversion on their own. Strictly speaking, a family in which one parent converts to the religion of the other is no longer an "interreligious" family, and there should be no possibility of disputes over the religion in which the children will be raised. Sometimes there are problems, though, because the children have relatives of different religions.

Reform and Reconstructionist synagogues will accept a child into their educational programs if either the father or the mother is Jewish. Temples affiliated with these movements should be the preferred choice of parents of differing religions who seek a Jewish education for their children. Both of these groups seek to make such children feel welcome in their synagogues and integrate them fully into their spiritual and cultural activities.

Parents who are able to set aside their ego involvement can use fairly objective factors in deciding on a religious identity for their children. While Christian churches and Reform and Reconstructionist synagogues are all supposed to welcome interreligious families, it unfortunately doesn't always happen that way. Some priests, ministers, and rabbis are not too comfortable with families of this type. Sometimes the curriculum of the church or synagogue school can be offensive to children of interreligious families. Sometimes lay people in the congregation, even without deliberately trying, can make children and parents of interreligious families feel uncomfortable and unwelcome. If you are a parent who takes the religious development of your children seriously, you should be aware of these facts and make an effort to visit the church or synagogue you are considering for your children. Talk with both the clergy and the teaching staff. When you have a "feel" for the community and sense that your children can get the kind of spiritual training that will enable them to grow, you will be able to join a parish or synagogue with peace of mind and the knowledge that your children will not be made to feel uncomfortable because of their special status.

"Train up a child in the way he should go, and when he is old he will not depart from it," the Bible says in Proverbs 22:6. This is the hope that all parents have for their children, but it is not always true where religious education is concerned. When they reach maturity, some children will give up the religious identity that was bestowed on them in favor of another one, and some will reject institutional religion altogether. But neither you nor society as a whole will be a loser if the religious path you chose for your children leads them to a love of the good, the true, and the beautiful, and of the God who is the Source of them all.

8

RELATING TO
YOUR IN-LAWS

The clichés that have grown
up around the relationships with in-laws are legion. Of
course they distort, but they obviously connect with
human experience, or those mostly forgettable stories
would not be so popular. One apt observer of human
society claims, "What distinguishes man from all other
animals is the fact of having in-laws. Perhaps man has
developed such a large brain in order to cope with a
complex kinship system." (Jay Haley, *Uncommon Therapy: The Psychiatric Techniques of Milton H. Erickson,* New
York: W. W. Norton & Co., Inc., 1973.)

Since parenting is so crucial to the kinship system
and the development of children to maturity, it is inev-

itable that potential for tension results from the encounter of a parent with his or her daughter/son-in-law. The unique memories of each person in a marriage are cherished by different kin. These memories create often unspoken expectations in the older generation that may never have had particular significance to their children. Because these expectations are often not communicated or even recognized, in-laws become easy scapegoats for family tensions. It is always much easier to resent your daughter-in-law for keeping your son from showing his love than to admit that your son doesn't respond as much as you would like. It is easier for a daughter-in-law to become angry at her mother-in-law for her intrusiveness than to confront her husband directly for not supporting her with an assertive response that would help his mother understand and maintain a noninterfering relationship. The couple is probably continuing a way of relating to the next generation that has been established through decades of practice.

When different religious heritages are added to this rich mixture, with all its potential for misunderstanding, we have the catalyst for a variety of reactions. Few families bring genuine insight or even a mature understanding of the heritage of the other's tradition. It must be learned and consciously addressed. This is no place for easy assumptions.

When Bill and Allison decided to marry, one of their first long conversations was about their relationships to each other's families. Their love for each other extended to the other's parents, brothers, and sisters in large part because they saw in the members of the other's family many of the same attributes that attracted them to each other. They could not help but be fond of those who had nurtured in love the one whom they each loved, but they knew that fondness, even love itself, could not bridge the potential distance that can emerge in marriage, especially an interfaith marriage.

Such issues as Bill and Allison faced, the potentials for difficulty they listed, and the strategies they agreed upon are the bases for many of the suggestions that follow. But the most important fact is that they raised their consciousness of the challenge by observation, by open communication, and by reaching a consensus concerning their life together and with their respective families.

When it comes to marriage, nothing can supplant an open and honest discussion leading to understanding and acceptance. In some situations, of course, no reconciliation is possible. In certain sectors of Orthodox Jewish tradition, the Jew who marries a person of another religious tradition is simply erased from the family and community. That is one way to solve the "in-law" challenge that few would cheerfully embrace. A few Christian sects would react similarly toward one of their own who married "outside the faith." But these are the exceptions. In most instances peace and harmony are the goals of all concerned. Parents are interested primarily in the happiness and well-being of their children. Their children's choice of spouse is accepted and respected even if they have reservations. Acceptance and respect are far more likely to prevail in an atmosphere of openness. In every marriage when care is given to nurturing the wider family relationships, the results are nearly always beneficial. An interfaith marriage simply enlarges the agenda.

Each marriage has its own special set of circumstances relating to intergenerational relationships. We will suggest some common in-law situations that need careful attention and will offer positive guidance in approaching whatever comes in a particular marriage relationship.

Hints about potential difficulties in an interfaith relationship often can come well before any commitment is made. When Bill came home from his first date with Allison, his parents asked what seemed to be an innocent question: "What church does Allison attend?" They had already noted that her last name sounded as though it might be Jewish. Another hint of possible future problems came the day Bill stopped by Allison's apartment. Her Jewish grandmother was visiting and sat across the room warily and silently observing him. He sensed that as far as she was concerned he was not all that welcome. Even families who genuinely feel they harbor no prejudice and count persons of different faiths among their dear friends suddenly exhibit a certain anxiety when their Christian or Jewish offspring begin dating persons of the other tradition. Don't ignore these signs. You may decide that it is not necessary to address the issue after the first date, but don't wait until you are ready to announce the engagement before positively discussing the issue. Your bringing it up can often help diffuse unspoken concerns before they grow out of proportion.

As your relationship continues and grows closer, both of you will want your parents to meet and know one another. The two of you enjoy each other and expect the same of your future in-laws. Some cautions should be observed. One often-overlooked cultural difference is that Christian and Jewish families may have different expectations about the role of in-laws in the family. Some Jewish families expect that their children's in-laws will become their close friends and participate in their social circle. This is not as readily assumed in Christian families. Most Catholic and Protestant families would not take for granted that a close social relationship would develop with in-laws unless they relate well together as friends. They would be together for special all-family occasions but may see one another socially only occasionally if at all. Jewish parents may be disappointed and hurt because of different expectations. A feeling of rejection can result when none was intended.

In planning the wedding festivities it is important that in-laws be informed of important but unfamiliar cultural and religious traditions. If they do not ask, their own son or daughter can help immensely by informing them both of the traditions and their expected roles in them. A Protestant father may be ill prepared for the expected toasting at the marriage reception dinner if he is not told in advance. Jewish parents may be surprised by the self-effacing behavior of Christian parents in some traditions. A major contribution you can make to your parents is to help them understand and be comfortable in another tradition.

Misunderstandings are most likely to occur in two situations: first, in connection with the major religious holidays, and second, around the birth of a child.

Early in marriage tensions may arise around religious holidays. Parents may resent the apparent competition for your time around religious holidays that come in close sequence. It may show up in unidentified anger at your spouse or in-laws if your parents feel threatened by new holidays or traditions that are foreign to them. The fact that busy people can celebrate only so many holidays and cannot simply double them means that couples must inevitably choose among the special occasions. One couple we interviewed stated that each of them had tolerated inappropriate behavior from their spouse's parents much better than from their own. They suggested that some of the stress in many intermarriages might have to do with sorting out the differences between oneself and one's own parents. It is helpful sometimes, when relating to difficulties with in-laws regarding holiday celebrations and other concerns, to step back and observe how you respond to your own parents with regard to the same issue in a different context.

Christianity and Judaism have basic practices that, if not carefully explained, cause discomfort to persons of other traditions. The birth of a boy may cause unspoken tension in Christian grandparents if they find the ritual circumcision of newborn boys distasteful. While they would probably ask their physician without hesitation to circumcise their own child for hygienic reasons, they may view the ritual act as almost barbarous. Christian in-laws invited to a grandson's circumcision may refuse to come or may make an excuse. In like manner, Christians need insight into the dimensions in their faith that offend many Jews; in this way each can understand and accept the other. A parallel in Christianity might be found in what appears to be undue emphasis on cruel and sadistic torture, namely, the nails driven into hands and feet, the sword piercing the side, and the hours of hanging on the cross in the New Testament description of the death of Jesus. Every cultural and religious tradition has practices that are so ingrained in the community's life that few view them as they may appear to someone from a different background.

It is while anticipating the birth of a grandchild that in-laws begin asking, if they haven't already, about the child's religious nurture. Even if they have been informed and intellectually accept the decision about their grandchild's religious upbringing, old fears and emotions may surface around the time of birth that would never be felt otherwise. If the parents are secure in their joint decision about their plans for their child, much of the possible tension can be reduced. Parents should not use the pressures of in-laws to delay or avoid a decision about the religion they wish to provide for their children. Even though it is not necessary to determine at the time of birth the tradition in which a child will be raised, delay beyond the child's fifth birthday often results in denying him or her one of the most vital heritages anyone can have. Few in-laws would want their grandchild bereft of any religious heritage. This does not preclude the great importance of giving one's child respect and knowledge of each parent's traditions, but we do state as forcefully as we can that so-called neutrality betrays parental responsibility and is the least desirable option.

Whatever decision is made regarding the religious nurture of your child, invite and include both sets of in-laws in the important occasions of that development. Be it Baptism, infant dedication, ritual circumcision,

Confirmation, Bar or Bat Mitzvah, or First Communion, make it, to the extent possible, an affair in which the whole family can be involved. In this way common memories are collected in the wider family, and you subtly build bridges of understanding and acceptance.

An infant girl, Amy, brought delight to Bill and Allison as the firstborn in their marriage. Deciding to nurture the child in the Christian tradition, they invited both sides of their family to the service of Baptism. In planning with his pastor, Bill suggested that his wife's family rabbi would perhaps respond positively to an invitation to participate with a blessing of the child in connection with the Baptism. (Allison's mother had already ascertained the rabbi's attitude.) The invitation was given and gladly accepted. At the Baptism Amy wore her father's baptismal dress, a white dress trimmed with lace that had been sewn by his grandmother and lovingly packed away twenty-five years ago by his mother. Three generations from Bill's side were celebrated. Allison's family rabbi, a friend of many years who had shared both joy and sorrow in their lives and who had participated in Bill's and Amy's wedding, gave a very special and personal blessing to the child from the Jewish tradition. In the party that followed everyone commented about how the experience had been made even more meaningful by affirming both heritages. As the years went by, Amy was raised in the church as a Christian, but at every milestone in her growth and development the family found creative ways to respect and celebrate her Jewish heritage. As she has matured, Amy expresses her religious life in the church but always cherishes her family's Jewish history as well.

Even with the best of intentions, unanticipated questions emerge. Grandparents may inadvertently cause tension simply by insensitivity to the decisions made by the parents for their children's growth and development. Just as a couple should show consideration for the feelings and attitudes of in-laws, so the in-laws need to be especially sensitive to the decisions the parents have made with regard to the religious training of their children. An example would be Christian grandparents giving a religious book to their grandchild without first securing the parents' consent. Those raising their children as Jews may not appreciate a religious book about Jesus. Parents who are raising their children as Christians may not think that a younger child is ready for a book about Jewish holidays. Parents have the right to have their wishes respected in this regard.

Beware, however, of becoming too rigid in attitude. Jewish parents, for instance, may not want their child's Christian grandparents to give him a Christmas present or, on the other hand, Christian parents may not cheerfully receive a Hanukkah gift for their child. Such attitudes are most unfortunate and, in our judgment, inappropriate. Surely grandparents should have the privilege of giving gifts to their grandchild at any time they choose. Who would deny grandparents this joy? If they are moved by the spirit of Christmas to give a gift, they should be able to, for their grandchildren should realize and appreciate that they are Christians; this is also true, of course, if they choose to give a Hanukkah gift because they are Jews. Either holiday is a wonderful time to give a present to a child, assuming that the gift itself is appropriate.

As in any extended family, sensitivity to the traditions and expectations of others is the hallmark of developing warm, friendly relationships. It can often be something as simple as inquiring about dietary restrictions and preferences when inviting in-laws to dinner. Your in-laws' discovery that you note and respond to their traditions and needs will go far in creating a sense of family togetherness across many of the so-called religious and cultural barriers. You should, of course, respect the religion and culture of others as you expect them to respect yours. An interfaith marriage does not need to blur the distinct heritage of either tradition. Those who claim that to honor the religion of another results in disrespect for their own do not have an adequate understanding of or security in their own traditions. Expect good relationships with your in-laws. Approach them openly and fondly. You love their offspring. Expect to love them. They won't be like your parents, but that's part of the joy of marriage. Your family multiplies in so many fascinating ways.

9

CEREMONIES OF GROWING UP

THE JEWISH LIFE CYCLE

When a Child Is Born

Interreligious families, like other families, want to know about the ceremonies the different religions prescribe for their children as they approach the various milestones that punctuate the pattern of their lives. Since we have already discussed the wedding, we now will consider the other events that mark the life cycle in Judaism.

In the beginning, of course, there is birth. If the

child is a boy, he is circumcised when he is eight days old. Circumcision is a surgical operation, the removal of the foreskin surrounding the head of the penis, and it has been practiced by many peoples since ancient times. Among the Jews it is derived ultimately from the belief of the Canaanites that everyone residing in the land of Canaan had to perform this rite as a sign of allegiance to the god of the land, an offering of a small portion of the body in order that the life of the child might be preserved. In the book of Genesis this Canaanite tradition is reinterpreted as a sign of the covenant between Yahweh and Abraham. All of Abraham's descendants are to follow the practice; God, in return, would give them the land of Canaan as an everlasting possession, and He would be their God. Because of its close association with the covenant made with Abraham, circumcision is called *brit mila,* "the covenant of circumcision," or simply *brit.*

The only Jewish males exempt from the obligation of circumcision are those whose life or health would be endangered by the operation, such as hemophiliacs. The operation, according to traditional practice, must be performed on the eighth day even if that day happens to be the Sabbath, Day of Atonement, or other Jewish holiday. The only acceptable reason for postponing the procedure past the eighth day is medical necessity; if a physician states that the operation should be delayed, then his instructions are followed. Ritual circumcisions are performed by a specially trained expert, a *mohel.* Orthodox and Conservative Judaism insist that a qualified *mohel* preside. Some Reform Jews, however, have a physician perform the circumcision as part of ordinary hospital procedure, usually the day after the baby is born. In such cases a rabbi might come to the family's home when the baby is eight days old to name and bless the child, or the blessing could take place as part of a Sabbath service in the synagogue.

While circumcision on the eighth day is a requirement for those who are born Jews, it does not have to take place on the eighth day if it is, in effect, part of the procedure by which someone is converted to Judaism. Circumcision as a conversion rite should not take place on a Sabbath or Jewish holiday, but should be scheduled at the convenience of the *mohel* in consultation with the family. Since a *mohel* is practically always an Orthodox or Conservative Jew, he will not regard the child born to a non-Jewish mother as Jewish; in this event the only basis on which he will participate is by construing the procedure as part of the conversion process, and some of the more rigid ones will not even participate on this basis. In spite of this, however, circumcision does *not* make one a Jew. If one is born a Jew, he bears that identity whether he is circumcised or not; and someone who is circumcised as part of the conversion procedure does not actually become a Jew until he reaches his thirteenth birthday, when religiously speaking he is an adult and can either accept or reject Judaism. The prayers and blessings that are part of the ordinary ritual make no reference to the religious identity of the child. They bestow a name upon him, plead for him to be shielded from evil and danger by virtue of the sign of the covenant that is placed within his flesh, and speak of the hope that he will grow up to enjoy the study of the word of God, a worthy marriage, and a lifetime of good deeds. The baby is given a drop of wine as part of the ceremony so that he can participate with his elders in the joy of the occasion, and then all partake of the meal of celebration.

Circumcision is practically universal for all Jewish male children, even those from families where there is little or no religious interest. In the United States circumcision is also common for non-Jewish male infants since it has been considered helpful to cleanliness and hygiene. Every twenty years or so, however, articles appear in newspapers and journals questioning the value of routine circumcisions performed for hygienic rather than religious reasons. Interreligious families should not be influenced by the periodic campaigns waged against the operation. Male infants who are fully Jewish or half Jewish should be circumcised either in a religious or a purely medical procedure unless a physician certifies that there is good reason for not doing so. In families where it is decided that children will be raised as Jews there can be no debate about such a decision. But, you might ask, why should the same decision be made by families who raise their children as Christians or who have left the religious identity of their children in abeyance until they have reached a more advanced age? The reason is that while circumcision for an infant is minor surgery that causes little or no pain, for an adult it is a painful and debilitating procedure. If there is even the slightest possibility that your child will want to assume a Jewish identity later in life, he should be circumcised as an infant. Since most American Christians are also circumcised, he will thus be in good company in either Jewish or Christian circles and will be spared the pain and discomfort of having to undergo the operation as an adult if he should, in later years, come to regard his lack of a circumcision as a stigma. The bulk of medical opinion continues to see hygienic value in circumcision, so on this basis also interreligious families should choose it for their infant sons.

Interreligious families who wish to arrange a religious circumcision for their sons should have no trouble engaging a *mohel* if the mother is Jewish. If the mother is not Jewish, they will have to find a *mohel* who will be willing to perform the procedure as part of the process of converting the child to Judaism. If you do not know where to find a *mohel*, you should contact a local rabbi who can put you in touch with one. Families who wish to have a physician perform the surgical operation should contact a Reform rabbi or other knowledgeable Jew who might be willing to perform a ceremony naming and blessing the child. This can be done either at home, in the context of a celebration for family and friends, or in the synagogue as part of the Sabbath service. Some rabbis make themselves available for these ceremonies to the public at large, while others will officiate only for members of their congregations. For this reason it is fortunate that a rabbi is not needed for this ceremony. Any Jew who knows how to read the ritual, even a relative, is eligible to officiate.

Why all these pages about the blessing of a son? Don't daughters deserve the same amount of attention? Of course they do, but there is no surgery involved when a daughter is born. Traditionally, daughters were named and blessed at a Sabbath service in the synagogue, but with the development of the Jewish feminist movement there has been a trend during recent years toward home ceremonies, complete with festive repast, similar to what is done when a boy is born.

If you have a daughter and wish her named and blessed in the Jewish manner, contact a rabbi to discuss whether he or she would perform such a ceremony at home or in the synagogue. If the rabbi is not receptive, then any knowledgeable Jew who can acquire a text for the ceremony is fully qualified to perform it.

There is no single tradition that governs all Jews with regard to the choice of children's names. Many Jews whose ancestry stems from northern Europe (Ashkenazic Jews) have the custom of always naming a child after a deceased relative. Sephardic Jews, on the other hand, those whose ancestry stems from the countries around the Mediterranean, have the custom of naming children after grandparents whether living or dead. Some Jews, however, who come from families where children are always named after deceased relatives have a superstitious dread of naming a child after anyone who is still alive. There can be many an emotional confrontation, even with Jewish families, when this issue arises. In an interreligious situation it can arise when one side of the family insists that a child be named only after the dead while the other follows a tradition of naming after the living. The solution has to be a compromise, of course, and since most parents bestow both a first and a middle name upon their children, the compromise is not too difficult. One name can be given according to one family's tradition, and the second name in accordance with the other family's.

According to most Jewish families, a child is named after someone if he or she bears the same Hebrew name or a similar one as the person being honored or memorialized. According to other Jewish families, a child is named after someone only if he or she is given the same American (or English) name or a similar one, in addition to the Hebrew name, as the person being honored or memorialized. Some families feel there should be a correspondence between Hebrew and English names, such as a similar meaning or, more often, the same initial sound. Other families feel there need not be any relationship at all between Hebrew and English names. Parents of newborn children have the option of following family tradition in these matters or, if they prefer, striking out on their own and giving their children whatever names they wish without paying heed to the past.

Coming of Age

Circumcision is an ancient ritual, going back to the very origins of the Jewish faith and people. Bar Mitzvah, however, is a fairly recent innovation, going back only to the medieval period. This celebration marks the coming of age, at thirteen, of a Jewish boy. The phrase means "son of the commandment," when one is obligated to take on the religious duties of an adult. It derives, of course, from the fact that thirteen is normally the age of puberty and that the young man is now qualified to fulfill the very first commandment given to the entire human race: "Be fruitful and multiply." The Bat Mitzvah ceremony for girls is only about fifty years old, but it has become quite popular among all the branches of Judaism other than Orthodoxy.

Unlike circumcision, which is an operation performed on a boy whether he likes it or not, the Bar Mitzvah and Bat Mitzvah rituals can be performed only with the consent of the child. They require the study of Hebrew, Jewish history, and theology. Bar and Bat Mitzvah rituals take place as part of the Sabbath service. Most synagogues require that young people fulfill a certain minimum number of years of formal religious school study before they are eligible for the ceremony. The ceremony itself sees the young person called up for the first time to the public reading of the Torah. He or she chants the benedictions before and after the reading of the biblical lesson and a few verses from the Torah scroll itself, and then chants the benedictions that accompany the reading of the lesson from the Prophets as well as the lesson itself. There is often a short speech by the Bar or Bat Mitzvah, followed by a blessing on the part of the rabbi. Though Bar and Bat Mitzvah ceremonies should take place in a synagogue, some families not affiliated with a congregation hire a private tutor, invite a group of family and friends over for a service, and hold the ceremony at home or other suitable location. While rabbis do not approve of this method, Judaism as a religious system has no objection since worship services can be held in any edifice or even outdoors and do not require the presence of a rabbi or any religious professional. (It should be noted that the description of the Bar and Bat Mitzvah ritual given here is applicable to all branches of Judaism except the Orthodox branch, where a girl would not be permitted to read from the Torah scroll. Some Orthodox synagogues do not permit any type of Bat Mitzvah ceremony while others seek to make various accommodations that, in their judgment, allow a girl to celebrate her coming of age in an appropriate way but do not contravene the rules of *Halacha* that prohibit a woman from leading a public worship service at which men are present.)

The Bar and Bat Mitzvah ceremonies are supposed to be spiritual in nature, reflecting on the part of the young person a certain amount of mature understanding of the religious tradition. To many people, however, the party following the religious service is of greater significance than the ceremony itself. Soon after its beginnings a century and a half ago, Reform Judaism developed the ceremony of Confirmation as a substitute for the Bar Mitzvah in the hope that it would provide a more spiritual emphasis to the occasion. Confirmation is a group exercise rather than a performance by an individual. It is tantamount to a graduation from the synagogue's religious school and in most cases involves a statement of faith or commitment on the part of those who are being "confirmed" in the religious tradition. Many Reform temples provide both Bar/Bat Mitzvah at age thirteen and Confirmation at age fifteen or sixteen. Relatively few young people, however, avail themselves of the opportunity to continue their studies and participate in the Confirmation ceremony. It is the Bar Mitzvah that has remained paramount as the Jewish coming-of-age ceremony, hallowed as it is by centuries; and it provides each family an opportunity to demonstrate the love and pride they share in the young man or woman.

An interreligious family that wishes a Bar or Bat Mitzvah ceremony for their child should, like any other family, investigate how many years of religious instruction a particular synagogue might require as preparation for the event. It should be understood that the service means the child has accepted Judaism as his or her own faith. Interreligious families in which the mother is Jewish should not have any problem in finding synagogues that will be willing to accept their child for religious instruction and for Bar Mitzvah. Families in which the mother is not Jewish, however, should restrict their inquiries to Reform and Reconstructionist synagogues since these groups are the only ones that will regard their children as Jewish.

When the Body Dies

Everyone must die eventually. If a Jew knows that he is near death, he should recite, "Hear O Israel, the Lord is our God, the Lord is One." There is no need to have a rabbi present when death occurs, but if a family is a member of a congregation or has a personal relationship with a rabbi, then that rabbi should be called, and if he is within reasonable distance, he will come. More important than the presence of a rabbi at the moment of death is the presence of the immediate family. Family members should consider it their supreme obligation to be on hand when death is imminent, particularly if the dying person is conscious and would be aware of their presence.

After death the body is ordinarily released to a mortuary and the funeral is scheduled, in most cases, one or two days after death. The only reason to wait longer is for the arrival of friends or relatives from out of town. (Since funerals and burials cannot take place on the Sabbath or major Jewish holidays, some services will be delayed for this reason as well.) A rabbi most likely will officiate at a funeral but, as in all other

Jewish ritual observances, any knowledgeable Jew is also acceptable. Funeral services are rarely scheduled at synagogues; they most often take place at a mortuary chapel (funeral home). The casket should be the simplest type available since all are supposed to be equal in death. In most instances flowers should not be sent to Jewish funerals. Charitable contributions in memory of the deceased or gifts of food to the bereaved family are acceptable.

Jewish tradition is specific about which relatives of the deceased are required to mourn a death in a ritual way. The following must do so: sons, daughters, father, mother, husband or wife, brothers, and sisters. In earlier times these mourners would rend their garments when a death occurred. Nowadays this is rare. Instead, just before the beginning of the funeral service the funeral director pins a black ribbon on the mourner's blouse or jacket and then cuts the ribbon. This ribbon is worn by the mourners for thirty days, except on the Sabbath, and is transferable from garment to garment. At the funeral psalms and prayers are recited, but the heart of the service is the eulogy of the deceased. Not only the person officiating, but friends and relatives are often encouraged to speak about the deceased and the spiritual legacy that he or she leaves behind. If a priest or minister was a friend, he also might deliver a eulogy.

Burial is the only way for a body to be disposed of in traditional Judaism, though cremation is acceptable in Reform Judaism as well. The interment service at the cemetery is very short, though in Orthodox Judaism it cannot be completed until after the casket has been lowered and the grave completely filled. After burial the mourners return home to the "meal of re-covery," usually bread and hard-boiled eggs, and there they remain for the seven days of mourning (*shiva*), during which time friends and family visit to console them. In more traditional families, worship services are held once or twice a day at the house of mourning for seven days. Also in traditional households the mirrors are covered (since they are a symbol of vanity), the mourners do not wear leather shoes, and the mourners do not sit on couches or soft chairs when visitors are present. At the end of the seven days (which some families reduce to three if circumstances prevent their staying away from work for all seven), the mourners resume their normal way of life but abstain from going to parties or amusements for the remainder of the thirty days during which they continue to wear the torn garment or ribbon.

Though formal mourning is ended after thirty days, the mourners should observe each anniversary of death by lighting a candle and attending the synagogue on that day or on the nearest Sabbath and participating in the "mourner's kaddish" (the word means sanctification). Many Jews do not realize it, but the kaddish itself has nothing to do with death or mourning. It is a doxology that begins: "Magnified and sanctified be His great name, in the world which He created by His will. May His kingdom come in your lifetime and in your day, and in the life of all the house of Israel, speedily and soon." The kaddish is recited several times at every public worship service. It became customary, though, for one kaddish at each service to be reserved for the mourners who were present so they could in this way affirm their faith in God and his redemptive power in spite of the tragedy they had undergone. The mourner's kaddish is recited during the thirty days of mourning and on the anniversary of death, but it should be recited for eleven months for a parent whenever a son or daughter is in attendance at a worship service. In this way the children are able to publicly affirm that extra measure of gratitude and devotion to the parents who brought them into being, and raised and sustained them.

A point of special concern to interreligious families is whether family members who are not Jewish can be buried with their Jewish relatives in Jewish cemeteries. This depends on what organization owns and operates the particular cemetery in question. Cemeteries operated by Reform synagogues or Jewish fraternal organizations unaffiliated with any religious denomination permit the burial in family plots of those who are not Jewish. (It should be noted, though, that most of these cemeteries would not permit non-Jewish symbols on gravestones.) Cemeteries operated by Orthodox synagogues or organizations will not permit the burial in their grounds of anyone who is not Jewish. If this matter is of concern to you, then it is best to make your burial arrangements far in advance of need, in a cemetery that has an open policy.

Nonsectarian cemeteries make no distinctions of religion concerning who might be buried in their grounds, and from a Jewish perspective there is nothing wrong with a Jew being buried in such a place. Christian cemeteries in general, both Catholic and Protestant, nowadays have no problem with the interment of a Jew in a family plot (though this was not always true).

THE CHRISTIAN TRADITION

The wondrous process of growing up can be beautifully marked by religious milestones, each of which becomes a major rite of passage. It is by these rites, as much as anything else in life, that we embrace a heritage that gives our lives both history and destiny. The ceremonies of growing up in the Christian tradition mark the major steps in a child's growth and development. In the Church these rites of passage become an individual's initiation into the faith. They are a door to a person's participation in the rich, spiritual life of Christianity. In nearly all churches, Catholic, Protestant, and Orthodox, three primary ceremonies mark the spiritual growth of the child: Baptism, Communion, and Confirmation.

Baptism

The sacrament of Baptism is central in the life of the churches, and in most traditions it is the child's first religious experience. While the sacrament can be offered individually or in a small family gathering, Baptism is most meaningful when it is celebrated in the presence of the community of faith, the congregation, at a principal Sunday service. Because Protestantism affirms that the whole congregation shares in "godparenting" the candidate for Baptism, the Sunday service celebration is preferred, though not mandatory. In Catholic parishes Baptisms may be performed either at a Sunday Mass or at a special Sunday afternoon service at which several families gather for the Baptism of their children. Baptisms may be performed in homes or in hospitals, but this is not encouraged in any tradition unless an emergency is involved.

In Baptism the naming of the child is often a significant part of the sacramental act. The name and birth date recorded on the baptismal certificate make it a legal document. In Christian tradition the name becomes more than just the symbol for the individual. Its heritage is identified with the person who bears it for life. The meaning behind the name is sometimes carefully studied and has much to do with the choice.

Catholics, Protestants, and Orthodox parents often choose a name for their child because of its importance in the Christian tradition. It may be a saint's name, thus giving the child another special day in his or her life, the day when that saint is remembered and celebrated by the Church. It may be a biblical name, a tradition preferred by many Protestants, out of either the Old or the New Testament. Names such as David, Rachel, Sarah, Joel, and so forth, are cherished in both Jewish and Christian traditions. Christians often name children after grandparents or other revered family members. The application of Junior, the Third (III), or the Fourth (IV), is a way of handing down the same name from father to son; this has continued in some families but is not as common as it was decades ago.

When Larry Golman and his wife, Arlene Robbins, discovered they were to be parents, they realized their first child's name would carry important messages to both families. Each would be looking for ways in which their grandchild would carry on some of the family tradition. Because theirs was an interfaith marriage, the families were more than a little sensitive about this. They said very little but watched and waited anxiously. Larry and Arlene discussed possible names for a few months prior to the baby's birth and determined that the baby, whether a boy or a girl, would bear at least one name from each family tradition. Their child was a boy, and they named him Benjamin Robbins Golman: Benjamin was the name of Larry's Jewish grandfather, and Robbins was Arlene's maiden name. As was the case with Larry and Arlene, a name that is creatively and sensitively selected can bring special joy and gratitude to both families.

Baptism is a sacrament celebrated only once in the life of a Christian and is the primary (first) step in becoming a follower of Christ and a member of the Church. Baptism among Catholics, most Protestants, and Orthodox traditionally is celebrated at a very early age, perhaps the first time the infant child is brought into the church. At the time of the Baptism the family and clergy usually gather around the baptismal font. The parents carry the child to be baptized and are accompanied by godparents, if any. Sometimes grandparents, brothers, and sisters also accompany the family. The parents make a faith commitment on behalf of the child and covenant to nurture the child in the Church and in the Christian faith. The godparents make a similar vow. In many Protestant churches the members of the congregation also act as godparents and recite a covenant to nurture this and all children with love and care. The priest or minister holds the child, names the infant, and then pours a small amount of water on the head, baptizing the child in the name of the Father, Son, and Holy Spirit. A significant group of Protestants, including Baptists, Disciples of Christ, and some Methodists, practice what is sometimes called "believers' Baptism"; it is celebrated for those who are able to make a mature affirmation of faith, usually at about age twelve.

Infant Baptism has a long and rich heritage and is surrounded by many cultural customs which, although not adding anything significantly religious to the ceremony, are cherished traditions. The scheduling of the rite at a time when most of the family can be present is important. Grandparents are welcome and encouraged to be present. The choice of godparents is carefully made because traditionally they share with the parents in the spiritual nurture of the child. Many churches require that the godparents be practicing Christians because of the vows they take with regard to the child's religious growth and development. One lovely tradition is the child's wearing a christening dress or outfit that has been passed down from generation to generation, perhaps one that had been hand sewn by a beloved elderly or deceased family member. After the Baptism at the church, families often gather for a traditional family dinner. In many traditions gifts are given to the child. The child's first step in faith has been taken.

In those traditions celebrating "believers' Baptism," the preferred time is following a period of nurture in a class of preparation. The recipient of Baptism, usually an early adolescent, first makes a personal affirmation of faith. Many of the churches practicing believers' Baptism baptize by immersion, which is an acceptable form (along with sprinkling or pouring) in any tradition. It is more dramatic because the candidate is completely immersed in water in the ceremony (special clothing is provided by the Church). Most scholars agree this is the way Baptism was first performed in the Church. It is an option in Catholic and almost all Protestant churches. In churches practicing believers' Baptism, a service of blessing and dedication is provided for infant children; it is similar to infant Baptism except that the actual sacrament is delayed until the child is mature enough to make his or her own faith commitment.

Certain seasons are often emphasized for Baptism. In the early centuries of the Church most Baptisms were celebrated on Easter eve. The Baptism experience symbolizes the death, burial, and Resurrection of Christ; thus Easter eve was considered the most significant time. In the Catholic Church the most beautiful ceremony of Baptism occurs on Holy Saturday (Easter eve) at the Easter vigil. Since the vigil ceremony is in the evening and rather elaborate in ritual and length, families are sometimes reluctant to choose that time. A baby's fussing in a lengthy service causes self-consciousness among the family. If possible, however, it is worth the effort to take part in what is a most beautiful ritual in the Catholic Church. Among Protestants the springtime season from Easter to Pentecost is often a time for Baptisms.

Baptism, in any tradition and whenever celebrated, is an "Easter" event. All the elements of the ritual are connected to the Church's celebration of Easter. All traditions include the welcome, the naming, the profession of faith, and the Baptism with water. The Catholic

173

Church also includes the signing with the cross and anointing with oil. The Church expresses its belief that all life, and especially the life of the person baptized, is a gift of God, and the gift of life is eternal. In all churches it is a primary sacramental act. In the Catholic Church it is the most important of the sacraments.

Over the centuries a widespread belief among Catholics was that there was no salvation without Baptism into the faith of the Church. This teaching, which was not supposed to be interpreted as denying the possibility of salvation for those who participate in other religious traditions, came to be associated with the concept of Limbo—that babies who died unbaptized were unable to enjoy full participation in the "beatific vision" because they, like all humans, had been born into the state of original sin. Today this teaching is accompanied, however, by a renewed emphasis on the true meaning of Baptism. The ritual signifies an act of faith on the part of the parents, godparents, the parish community, and the whole Church that a child in this way becomes a member of God's family and shares His life. The sacrament today should be received not to rescue an infant from Limbo, but to reflect the conviction that God's love and will for salvation extend through the child, the parents, the parish, and the Church to embrace the entire human family.

In most Christian traditions Baptism should take place in the church of the parish where the parents live. Because it is the formal entrance into the community of the Church, the child begins his or her Christian growth in the community that will offer the nurture and support needed to become a mature Christian. Sometimes the parish church of the godparents, grandparents, or where the husband and wife were married is suggested by the family, but the Baptism should take place where the child will grow to maturity in religious practice.

Baptism is as much a celebration by the whole Church as it is for the child. Just as the parents give life to a child, the godparents, the community of relatives and friends, and the congregation join with them in giving faith to the child in Baptism. The question of when to baptize a child often depends on the Church tradition of the parent. Those traditions that baptize older children and adults reserve the sacrament until the individual achieves adequate maturity to make his or her own profession of faith. The majority of churches that practice infant Baptism point out that just as you do not ask a child if it wants beer or milk to drink—you give it milk—so, too, with the faith. As the child grows in the practice of its faith, he or she will mature in the knowledge of God as it is known in the family.

In most Christian traditions the celebration of Baptism assumes that the child will be nurtured in the Christian faith. Baptism is almost universally preceded by a confession of faith in Christ either by the candidate or on behalf of the infant by the parents. Many churches will recommend to parents who have not yet determined the faith in which they will nurture their child that they wait until they have decided specifically on a Christian heritage before having the child baptized. However, nearly all priests and ministers will be pleased to participate in a special liturgy of blessing and thanksgiving for the child.

Coming of Age

Other sacramental acts—Confirmation, Communion and, in the Catholic Church, Reconciliation or Penance (Confession)—follow Baptism. In all Protestant traditions Confirmation follows a period of study (usually from six weeks to a year or more) in which the child studies the nature of faith and the Church. Confirmation classes (or classes in preparation for Baptism) usually are scheduled when the child is about twelve years of age. Confirmation is also a major time in the life of the youth. In most churches Confirmation is considered one of the first adult decisions an individual makes, and the adolescent's rite of passage to a more mature faith is celebrated. A public profession of faith and often the answering of questions about the nature of faith are parts of the Confirmation experience. In Catholic and Episcopal churches Confirmation is imposed by a bishop who accepts the candidate into the community of faith and confers the gifts of the Holy Spirit. At this time the confirmand affirms the faith received in Baptism. Confirmation is a major celebration with family members present. Once again gifts are bestowed on the youth, and often a special family feast is planned. While Confirmation in many Western countries is received mostly by teenagers, in Eastern Catholic rites and in some Latin countries, as well as in Orthodox Christianity, it is conferred on very young children along with Baptism.

First Communion in the Catholic and some Protestant churches is taken at age seven or eight. In other churches it may follow immediately or soon after Confirmation. An increasing number of Protestant churches, however, are encouraging children to receive Communion before they reach the age of Confirmation. Communion is a church "family" tradition, and many feel that young children should not be denied the experience. Whenever First Communion is celebrated, in most traditions it is significant and elaborate. It is usually preceded by some weeks of instruction in the meaning of the sacrament. New clothes for the child, often white, are customary in some ethnic traditions. Extended families gather, and it becomes a holiday feast with special gifts for the child.

The Eucharist is celebrated as part of every Mass in Catholic and Orthodox churches. Among Protestants the practice varies, from the Episcopal and Disciples of Christ traditions with Eucharistic celebrations at almost every service to many others that celebrate Communion monthly or sometimes only quarterly. Most Christians meet regularly to "break the word of Scripture and the bread of life." They grow in faith and celebrate the mystery of Christ's presence in their lives. The ritual expresses that we can and do live by faith in communion with God and other people.

In Catholic churches and in a few other traditions another sacrament that children experience as they grow up is called Reconciliation (Confession); this expresses ritually that we all share in the mercy of God and have shared in victory over sin. A person who is sorry for sins committed confesses them to a priest and receives absolution, restoring the penitent to the bonds of faith and to the community of the Church and God. The person is reconciled with the Church through this sacrament. There is an increasing emphasis in Catholicism on the confession of social sins, such as racist acts or attitudes, as part of the process of Reconciliation. A Catholic with a serious problem of conscience is expected to seek the sacrament of Reconciliation before receiving Communion. It thus becomes a repeated pattern in the Catholic's life of faith. Confession in most Protestant traditions is a corporate act included in the Sunday liturgies voiced together by the congregation.

Catholics recognize that in the sacrament of Reconciliation there is a delicate growth of conscience. We all know that around the age of reason children usually know the difference between mistakes and accidents, wrongs and sins. Religious education programs in the parishes usually guide them to a point where they can understand these things and receive the sacrament in accordance with their tender age.

Among Protestants a major part of growing up Christian is the Sunday Church School. Sunday School programs in some churches run from cradle to grave, but the most important period is from preschool through high school. Sunday School classes usually are scheduled for an hour before, after, or during the Sunday liturgical service. Volunteer teachers teach the Bible and the themes of Christian faith. Sunday Schools often have special graduations, parent events, and other occasions when family participation is encouraged. If parents elect to nurture their child in a Protestant tradition, part of the experience surely will include enrollment in a Sunday School program. Connected to Sunday Schools are often well-planned youth programs of fellowship, service, retreats, and camping.

When Death Comes

Death is a fact of life but, from a Christian perspective, it is a milestone on a much longer pilgrimage. Although some Christian traditions define death in specifics, all agree that life is more than the sum of its parts. God, who creates His children in love, does not abandon them in death. The Resurrection of Christ is what gives Christians this hope.

When death approaches, many Christians will want to "make their peace with God." Most traditions offer rites that provide for this. In the Catholic Church the sacrament of Anointing the Sick offers the individual the opportunity of Confession and Communion. Catholics are encouraged to receive this sacrament even when they do not anticipate death. A priest will provide the rite for anyone who is seriously ill so that he or she might gain encouragement and strength for recovery. Among Protestants the procedure is less formalized, but a minister is often called upon to pray with and bring Communion to the sick. Most Protestants do not believe that a confession of sins is needed for God to forgive a dying person. A minister, therefore, will not ask for such a confession unless the individual indicates that he wishes to offer one.

After death the body is usually taken to a mortuary. Funeral practices vary, though Protestant funerals take place in funeral chapels more than in churches. A Catholic in good standing, however, will always be buried from a church, preferably the one in which he or she worshiped during life; the liturgy is called the Mass of Christian Burial. Some Protestant ministers recommend an immediate burial of the body, to be followed by a memorial service in the church at a later date. While this is an increasing practice, most people still prefer the traditional funeral.

A minister usually presides at a Protestant memorial service or funeral, but in many churches any informed Christian may do so. The liturgy contains prayers, Scripture readings, and some specific comments about the deceased (but usually not a eulogy). Both Catholic and Protestant traditions accept cremation as well as burial in or above ground. An increasing number of Protestant churches, especially in urban centers, include a columbarium in their facilities for the interment of ashes. In the case of an interreligious family, neither the Catholic nor the Protestant tradition has any objection to the burial of a Christian in a family plot in a Jewish cemetery.

Mourning practices among Christians vary according to the particular community. In most of the northern and midwestern United States, the family gathers at the funeral home a day or so before the service, and friends come to express sympathy and concern. In the South, families usually remain at home to receive callers, and only a few persons go to the mortuary. Flowers may be sent to either the home or the mortuary. Increasingly, memorial gifts to charitable programs or institutions are given in the name of the deceased, often in lieu of flowers. In Catholic practice, Masses in memory of the deceased may be arranged at any parish church.

Following interment, the mourners return home, where the family and close friends might share a common meal. It is customary for friends to bring gifts of prepared food for this meal. Most people do not immediately return to a normal round of activity after a death, but the practice varies considerably. Recent generations have also given up traditional mourning clothing.

Because there is no established pattern of mourning practice among many Christians, one must be sensitive to the needs of individual persons in mourning. One should not hesitate to invite a family member of a deceased person to an appropriate function within a week or so of the funeral. Before that time, a personal visit to the home is usually preferred.

Many Protestant parish churches provide special times in their liturgies during the year for the remembrance of the dead. The Sunday nearest All Saints' Day (November 1) is often chosen, or sometimes New Year's Eve or New Year's Day.

What Should We Do?

We have been fairly detailed about the ceremonies that involve the Jewish life cycle, the Catholic sacraments that are conferred as a person passes through the various stages of growth in the life of the Church, and the Protestant tradition. But we have probably not answered the question that you have uppermost in your mind: What should *we* do? If you are an interreligious family, should your child have a Baptism or a circumcision, a Christian Confirmation or a Bar Mitzvah? Grandparents on each side are cheering us on, you say, to have one ceremony but not the other. Friends counsel us to have neither so that nobody will be "offended." But just as we wanted a religious ceremony for our wedding, so, too, do we want a religious ceremony for our child. What should we do?

The answer that we would give you is this: If both of you have decided on the religion you wish your child to bear while he or she is growing up, then you should seek the ceremonies of this religion. If you have agreed that your child is to be Jewish, then he or she should have a Jewish naming ceremony, be enrolled in a Jewish Sunday or Hebrew school, and at age thirteen have a Bar or Bat Mitzvah celebration. If you have agreed that your child is to be Christian, then he or she should have a Baptism (if the denomination is one that baptizes infants), be enrolled in the Sunday school or catechism class, and at the proper time receive First Communion and Confirmation. For people who know what religious direction their children will take, the choice of ceremonies is not too difficult. If some grandparents and other relatives are "offended," that is unfortunate. If there is effective communication on both sides, it should be possible to mollify hurt feelings.

What should you do, however, if you have not decided on a single religion with which your child will identify? What if you want to give your child an equal involvement with both Judaism and Christianity? What if you hope to agree on a religious destiny for your child but want to wait until he or she is older before doing so—but at the time of birth you wish a religious ceremony to welcome your child into the human community? Fear not, for you are not alone. Many interreligious families are in your situation. The dilemma is not insoluble. Just as love and consideration for each other helped you to decide what to do at the time of your wedding, so love and consideration for each other can help you to welcome your child into the world in a religious way.

Our suggestion is that you seriously consider having the ceremonies of both Judaism and Christianity when your child is born. The ceremonies do not cancel each other out. They give both sides of the family an equal opportunity to celebrate, and they can demonstrate to those who participate the richness of the two religious traditions. For this reason we recommend that, if you have not yet reached a decision, you give your child a ritual circumcision or Jewish naming ceremony along with a Christian Baptism or other blessing. (Most priests and ministers consider Baptism an irrevocable introduction to Christianity, though some do not. For this reason you cannot insist on a Baptism if the priest or minister does not think it is proper. It is likely he will be willing to extend another form of Christian blessing to the child. Similarly, ministers of churches who do not believe in infant Baptism for anyone as a matter of religious principle are often willing to bestow some form of Christian benediction on a newborn child.)

While we are sympathetic to the concept of two religious ceremonies when a child is born, we strongly counsel against any attempt to send a child to both Jewish and Christian schools of religious instruction when he or she is old enough to be formally educated. Celebrating the holidays of both Judaism and Christianity in your home is fine. Attending services of worship in both synagogues and churches as a family—by all means. But by the time your child is old enough for religious instruction in a school setting, you should have decided which way you wish your child to go—to be committed to either Judaism or Christianity as a personal faith and way of life. Sending your child to two forms of religious instruction at the same time can only sow confusion and, perhaps, lay the ground for neurosis in later life. For this reason it cannot be Bar Mitzvah and Christian Confirmation. It has to be Bar Mitzvah *or* Christian Confirmation. Bar Mitzvah is the culmination of a program of Jewish instruction and means that the young person regards himself or herself as a committed Jew. A Christian Confirmation is the culmination of a program of Christian instruction and means that the young person regards himself or herself as a Christian. Neither ceremony implies a rejection of the other half of his ancestry. If, as parents, each of you can show love and consideration to your partner and to your respective religious heritages, so can your Christian child demonstrate love and appreciation for his Jewish heritage, or your Jewish child for his Christian heritage. If he loves you, he will also love what you are.

Mark and Barbara are the parents of twins, a boy and a girl, who are now ten years old. Before they were born it had been decided that they should be welcomed into the world with both Catholic and Jewish ceremonies. Alan, the boy, was medically circumcised in the hospital and, when both were eight days old, a rabbi and a priest came to the family home for the religious rites. The priest read a passage from the Scriptures and gave a short homily. The rabbi conferred names on Alan and Gloria, not only in English but also in Hebrew. (Alan's Hebrew name is Abraham, Gloria's is Yochebed, the name of the mother of Moses). Then the priest and rabbi together invoked the biblical blessing on the children: "The Lord bless you and keep you. The Lord cause His face to shine upon you and be gracious unto you. The Lord lift up His face toward you and grant you peace." All the grandparents were present, as well as assorted aunts, uncles, and cousins. What was memorable about the ceremony, besides the warm and loving spirit that pervaded the household, was Gloria squirming in her mother's arms so much that she almost knocked the wineglass out of the rabbi's hand as he was pronouncing her name.

When the twins were about six years old, Mark and Barbara realized they had to make a decision about the religious education of their children. They visited the Catholic church and the Reform synagogue in their neighborhood, and met with the clergy at both institutions. They came to the conclusion that the synagogue offered the preferred environment for their children and for the family. When the twins reached the age of nine, they were enrolled in the Reform synagogue's religious school, meeting on Sunday mornings and one afternoon during the week. Gloria and Alan will be ready for a joint Bar and Bat Mitzvah celebration when their thirteenth birthday comes along. The temple congregation is looking forward to this with more than the usual enthusiasm since it will be the first time for this congregation that twins will be celebrating such a service. Mark, Barbara, and all their relatives also await the day, for they anticipate that the spirit of love and acceptance apparent when their twins were born will be on hand once again, this time making itself felt within an even larger circle of family and friends.

10

FACING YOUR
POTENTIAL
PROBLEMS

The approach we have taken in this book has been to "accentuate the positive," building on the fact that in today's world there is more that unites Jews and Christians than divides them. We have attempted to show that marriage between Jews and Christians can bring happiness and fulfillment, that those in such marriages need not give up their faith commitments, and that children growing up in interreligious families can turn out to be as well adjusted and culturally enriched as others by their dual heritage. Nonetheless, we have to admit that some people will encounter problems within an interreligious marriage. In fact, there are some people who should never even contemplate an interreligious marriage because their outlook is such that they can find happiness only with someone whose belief system and religious practices are the same as theirs. They may be very fine people, and they may even fall in love with a person whose religious commitment is not the same, but marriage to someone of a different faith is something they should avoid. If you think you might fall into one of the categories we will now discuss, we urge you to contact a competent counselor before getting too deeply involved in an interreligious relationship.

THE FUNDAMENTALIST CHRISTIAN

Jeff and Adele, both Christians, finally broke up because Adele's fundamentalist background made her suspect that Jeff's more open, liberal outlook was not true to Scripture. She believed literally in the Genesis story of God's creating the heavens and earth in only seven days. When Jeff suggested that this was a myth describing a great religious truth about a creator God but not a scientific description of beginnings, Adele was devastated. Because she was threatened by Jeff's position, their relationship deteriorated. Adele was afraid Jeff was not a true Christian.

Sometime later Adele began dating David, a Jew, and for a while it seemed their faith differences would not cause difficulty. Adele's literalist approach to Scripture allowed her to think of David as one of "God's chosen people," but with time doubts emerged that she could not put aside. A verse in the Gospel of John, "No man comes to the Father except through me (Jesus)," meant to her that no one could relate to

God except one who had, in her words, "confessed Jesus Christ as Lord." If David and Adele married and had children, Adele believed they would not only have to be baptized and nurtured as Christians but would also be expected at some point in their lives to have a personal "born again" experience of Jesus Christ as Lord and Savior. Otherwise, how could Adele be sure that they were indeed "saved" by God? Concerned not only about her unborn children but also about David's spiritual destiny, Adele's fundamentalism drove a wedge between them. Adele's understanding of faith prevented her from accepting both David's Jewishness and Jeff's liberal Christianity. Someone like Adele should not consider marriage to a Jew, nor should a Jew consider marriage to someone like Adele.

An interreligious family has to be based on mutual respect, a respect not only for each other but also for each person's background. No one should ever marry with the intention and expectation of "changing" a partner in any major way, and this certainly should include the intention to change a spouse's religious outlook. An interreligious marriage can succeed only if both parties enter into it with the conviction that each is indeed already righteous and acceptable in the sight of God—the Jew through his or her Judaism and the Christian through his or her Christianity.

CERTAIN TYPES OF JEWS

Just as a committed fundamentalist Christian should avoid marriage to a Jew, so, too, are there certain types of Jews who should avoid marriage to a Christian. Those who believe in and practice Orthodox Judaism, including the prohibitions imposed by Halacha (Jewish law as interpreted by the Orthodox rabbinate), are to be numbered among those who should not contract such a marriage. There are Jews who are not fully Orthodox in either belief or practice who should stay away from such marriages as well. The influence of the Orthodox way of thinking is felt beyond the bounds of those who lay claim to the title "Orthodox"; there are some who belong to other branches of Judaism, or who are completely secular and have no synagogue tie at all, for whom marriage to a Christian would be a grave mistake. Such people might be . . .

. . . *those who think that intermarriage is a sinful act.* Anyone who believes that God is displeased by the marriage of a Jew to a non-Jew and that the basic and primary mission of the Jewish people is to remain separate from all other peoples on the face of the earth should not marry a Christian unless he or she is a masochist who seeks psychic pain and punishment out of some private motivation unrelated to the marriage. (Some who hold this conviction apply it only to marriages in which children are likely to be produced and see nothing wrong or sinful in a companionate marriage to a Christian when both are up in years.)

. . . *those who think that intermarriage is a betrayal of their ancestors.* The family or tribal aspect of Judaism is very important to many Jews, and there is an appreciable number who abstain from marriage outside the group because they regard this as the most significant way they can demonstrate their love and loyalty to the line of their ancestors that goes back to biblical antiquity. The fact that one's parents oppose a marriage should not in itself prevent its consummation since most parents are apt to find something wrong with their child's choice of a mate even if he or she is of their own religious persuasion—unless it is that rare instance of a marriage arranged "the old-fashioned way," by the parents themselves. Though in this age of individualism many men and women are able to marry without their parents' wholehearted approval, it is quite another matter to feel that one's ancestors look upon the union with condemnation or lamentation, or both. This feeling often arises in the children of Holocaust survivors for they, even more than other Jews, are likely to be conscious of the tragic burden of the past that they can never escape. Therefore, a Jew who feels that an interreligious marriage is a betrayal of his ancestors should think long and hard about contracting such a marriage. Some are able to go through with it on the condition that their children be raised as Jews. In this way there is no betrayal, for the heritage of the ancestors is being transmitted into the future.

. . . *those who believe in observing the Jewish dietary restrictions because they sanctify and separate the Jewish people.* There are many Jews who were raised not to eat certain foods, such as pork and shellfish. Since they never acquired a taste for these foods as children, they prefer not to eat them as adults. Such an attitude does not disqualify them from a happy and satisfying interreligious marriage. People of all backgrounds have various tastes and preferences in foods. There is, however, a smaller number of Jews who embrace the conviction that the foods prohibited by the Jewish dietary laws are inherently unclean. Most people with this attitude are Orthodox, but some are not. Even though they may be very liberal about other aspects of Jewish religious practice, they hold that the basic prohibitions of the Jewish dietary laws should be preserved because the Jewish people must remain true to its inherent nature; which is to say, holy, pure, and uncontaminated by uncleanliness. One who thinks along these lines is better off not entering into an interreligious marriage because a very thin line separates that conviction from the conviction that certain people are inherently unclean for you and your people. A marriage must be based on the conviction that both partners are equally pure and holy in terms of the inherent nature that each possesses, and there should be no spiritual impediment to their coming together in union.

... *those who are unable to accept the celebration of Christmas in their home.* Many Jews enjoy various aspects of the Christmas holiday, but there are a number who do not, who find it either impossible or extremely difficult, in a deeply rooted emotional way, to accept the presence of a Christmas tree, holiday decorations, and observances in their own home. Christians, on the other hand, even those who are far from religious involvement, have an emotional tie to the Christmas season and everything that goes with it. It is unfair, in an interreligious home, for any impediment to be placed in the way a Christian celebrates Christmas, so it follows that a Jew who is unable to accept a Christmas celebration in his or her home should abstain from an interreligious marriage.

SENSITIVITY TO HUMAN NEEDS

Most American Christians are not fundamentalists who believe that one can be "saved" only through belief in Christ as a personal savior. Most American Jews, particularly those of marriageable age, do not look upon intermarriage as sinful or a betrayal of their ancestors, and they neither observe the Jewish dietary prohibitions nor object to Christmas celebrations. It is therefore normal to expect that there will be a great many marriages between Christians and Jews and that, on purely practical grounds unrelated to religious doctrine, there is no reason for objection to be raised to them. It should be assumed, though, that there will be instances of tension and stress within interreligious families that will seem on the surface to have a religious component. In most cases this will not be true. All families have arguments and interludes of unpleasantness. An interreligious family need have no more and no less than families in which the husband and wife have grown up in the same church.

Dan had grown up in a family in which neither he nor any of his three brothers had ever made a major decision without discussing the issue with both parents. His marriage to Adelaide, a New England Protestant, had received the approval of his Jewish parents, even though they had expressed their disappointment that he would be moving some distance away from them. Shortly after the marriage Dan had an opportunity to make a major career change. He decided to do so after discussing it with his wife but without asking his parents' advice. They were informed after the fact. Though she had never raised the matter of the religious difference before, Dan's mother began a constant drumbeat of complaint, both by telephone and by letter, about "Christian women who want to separate Jewish men from their parents, and from their religion as well." Of course this was not the issue at all. Dan's mother was unwilling to "let go" and refused to recognize that he was now at a point in his life when parental consent was no longer necessary or advisable. She displaced her anger at her son's new independence by directing it at his wife and her religious background. If Adelaide had been Jewish, Dan's mother would have been just as resentful but would have had to find some other personality trait to criticize. Dan and Adelaide were wise enough to realize what was really involved in their situation, and eventually Dan's mother quieted down too.

It is helpful for couples to recognize that marital conflicts, as well as matters involving parents, in-laws and other extended family members, do not always lay the real issues on the table. More often than not, marital conflicts reflect unresolved problems of relationships with parents or other family members brought into the marriage as "baggage," and one or both partners have to trip over this baggage that lies strewn about the psychic landscape. In many cases psychotherapy is necessary for the health of a marriage, but in many more instances all that is needed is for both partners to realize that problems are not always what they seem to be on the surface. Husbands and wives need to be sensitive to the family background from which their partners come and to realize that many of the resentments and complaints expressed should really be directed at other family members (though in most cases this would be neither possible nor advisable). An interreligious situation provides additional opportunities for resentments to be expressed, but people who love each other are able to transcend their difficulties if they recognize what is really involved. We wish to emphasize, though, that no spouse should say in the course of an argument, "I realize that you are behaving this way because you have a problem with your mother." Though this may very often be true, some truths are best left unsaid unless the context is the correct one for their enunciation.

Just as we can better tolerate each other when we understand the family background from which we stem, so, too, is life more pleasant when we appreciate that stress in general can take its toll of our usual capacity to tolerate others and their idiosyncrasies. When life is running along smoothly we accept and even enjoy the fact that others are different from ourselves, with their own tastes and preferences. When life is not treating us as kindly as we would like, however, we are more apt to lash out at those with whom we live and resent the differences in tastes and preferences that distinguish them from us.

Susan and Anthony had been married for six months, and she was looking forward to bringing him to the Passover Seder at her parents' house. Three days before the holiday, however, he was laid off from his job, and the prospect of his being recalled to work did not look very good. The day before the Seder, Anthony told his wife he would not be going; he had too much on his mind and did not feel like participating in a religious function he knew little about, with a group of people some of whom he did not know at all. Susan and her mother were both disappointed, but they understood what Anthony was going through and knew that his absence did not mean he had turned "anti-Jewish." Susan brought home a selection of the foods that were served so that he would know he was indeed missed and that the family remembered him even in the midst of its celebration. Susan was mature enough to understand that stress can make a person less tolerant of others and their activities, and Anthony appreciated her understanding of him and his needs.

It is when we get angry at each other that we are most likely to put aside the innate understanding we have for the needs of those we love. It is almost superfluous to say it, but of course an interreligious family has to take special care during the heat of an argument to avoid criticism and denunciation that is couched in religious or ethnic terms. Because the U.S. is made up of so many ethnic or religious groups, it has been a tradition of long standing for people to make jocular reference to these distinctions. In anger, however, these references are not always so funny. Though they often do not reflect any deep disdain or dislike for the individual or the ethnic or religious group, these references should be avoided in argument. It is one of the ways we show our sensitivity to the ones we love.

When we marry and commence to focus our primary energy on our relationship with our spouse, we of course continue to love our parents and wish to show them the same kindness and consideration we did before. More and more parents are learning to accept interreligious marriage and, as time goes on, there will be fewer and fewer "horror stories" about irrational and emotional reactions from parents when they learn that an offspring is about to marry someone of a different religion. If, however, your parents are still unwilling to accept the decision you have made, you will want to continue to love them and show them kindness and consideration. This does not mean you will necessarily give in to their demands, but you should assure them as vigorously as you can that your marriage does not mean a rejection of them.

Helping parents to accept an interreligious marriage may sometimes be strenuous and time-consuming. "When parents consider their son's or daughter's marriage a family or personal loss, they may have to engage in painful processes of working through that involve such stages as denial, bargaining, anger, guilt and, at last, acceptance. An understanding son or daughter will be caring, patient, and facilitating as his or her parents go through this process." (Man Keung Ho, *Building a Successful Intermarriage between Religions, Social Classes, Ethnic Groups or Races*. St. Meinrad, Indiana: Abbey Press, 1984.) As we must be sensitive to the human needs of the person we marry, so, too, must we be as sensitive as we can to the needs of the parents on whom we were dependent for so long.

ETHNIC CONSIDERATIONS

Besides the general sensitivity that people should show to each other out of an understanding of their basic human needs, interreligious families should also be aware of ethnic factors that may affect personality development and patterns of human interaction. In fact, when people bring up examples of family conflict and turmoil that they attribute to religious difference, they more often than not are referring to strictly ethnic factors that have nothing to do with religion as such. Few indeed are the arguments that husband and wife have about theology. The problems Jews and Christians married to each other most often encounter are the same ones an Irish man or woman married to an Italian will have, though both may be Catholic. Each culture encourages various modes of behavior in response to particular situations, and sometimes these modes of behavior come into conflict. As has been said, "Ethnicity patterns our thinking, feeling, and behavior in both obvious and subtle ways. It plays a major role in determining what we eat, how we work, how we relax, how we celebrate holidays and rituals, and how we feel about life, death, and illness." (Monica McGoldrick, *Ethnicity and Family Therapy*. New York: Guilford Press, 1982.)

An appreciation of the role that ethnicity plays in human interaction is very important, but it is equally important to avoid stereotyping. Though many Jews have a close tie to their mothers, not all of them do. Though many "WASPs" prefer to keep their personal problems to themselves instead of turning to others for sympathy or guidance, not all of them do. Though many Italians take great delight in laughing and singing around a festive dinner table, not all of them do. As time goes on, what are perceived as distinctive traits of various ethnic groups will merge into something more amorphous. The influence exerted by television, and American culture in general, will likely bring into being a population in which Greeks, Jews, Norwegians, Blacks, and Asians, as well as people growing up in the North, South, East, and West, will be nearly indistinguishable one from the other as far as behavioral traits are concerned. This process has been going on for some time, so no one should be surprised if people do not always behave in the ways we might have come to expect based on their ethnic ancestry. An understanding of what ethnicity can transmit, however, is extremely helpful to people who deal with others from a different background. It is especially helpful in a relationship as close and intimate as marriage.

Henry, of British American ("WASP") descent, is married to Susan, a Jew. They have a son, David, who recently celebrated his fifteenth birthday. In the Jewish family in which Susan grew up the pattern was to attempt to "hold on" to adolescent children as long as possible. Though her parents realized her brothers eventually had to strike out on their own, a process often styled "individuation," they wished to keep them within the bosom of the family and protect them from the vicissitudes of the world. In Henry's family, on the other hand, the tradition was for boys David's age to earn their own spending money and put away savings for college during their spare time. Henry encouraged David to get a job as a drugstore delivery boy, using his bicycle on the job during some of the most congested traffic hours of the day. Susan could not understand this. Why would his own father want to endanger David in this way? Henry, however, thought that sending David to this particular job was a way to develop his independence and maturity. Young men have grown up since time immemorial learning to face and overcome challenges, he thought, and maneuvering a bicycle through afternoon traffic is a useful talent that should be developed. The differences between Susan and Henry have nothing to do with religion as such, though a typical Jewish family pattern may be to want to protect one's children for as long as possible, while a typical WASP family pattern may be to encourage independence and initiative in children as soon as possible. Each parent "loves" his child with the same intensity, but has a different way of showing it. They should discuss the issue at hand calmly and rationally, and make a decision based on the objective factors involved.

Just as a Jew and a WASP might have different philosophies about child rearing, so might partners in a Jewish-Irish marriage. Many Jewish parents believe in praising their children for their accomplishments, whether large or small. Irish parents, however, are sometimes sparing with praise or compliments. (Some attribute this to the emphasis on human sinfulness that was long present in Irish religion. Also, the Irish were dominated for many years by foreign rulers who limited their opportunities for success and advancement. In response, Irish parents decided that the aims and hopes of their children should best be left at a low level in order to avoid disappointment when they could not be fulfilled.) A Jew with an Irish spouse may encounter no major problems in their relationship until a child is born. If the Jew was used to being complimented by parents almost from birth and notices the Irish spouse makes little or no fuss over their child, the Jewish partner may assume they are not sharing the same degree of love and pride in their child. This, of course, would be false. (In this instance, though, it is advisable that the trait of not complimenting be discarded. Family workers agree that children who grow up in an atmosphere of praise for their accomplishments are likely to be happier and more productive than those who do not.)

Some who are involved in Jewish-Italian marriages feel that their unions should not even be styled "intermarriages" since the family patterns of both groups are often so similar as to be indistinguishable. In both communities the family constitutes a primary orientation, not only the nuclear family of father, mother, and children but also the larger extended family. In both communities there is a great emphasis on the family's coming together for various festivities and the consumption of many different types of foods that have been prepared for the occasion. It used to be said that Italian Americans did not have too great an interest in higher education; this would be in contrast with the traditional Jewish focus on education. This, however, is certainly not true today. Italians, like Jews, are numerous in the universities and the learned professions, seeing education as a primary avenue for upward mobility, personal growth, and cultural enrichment.

Though Italian-Jewish marriages are very likely to be happy and fulfilling for both spouses, problems may arise out of ethnic behavior patterns. As has been noted, "bragging, dramatic impersonation either by impromptu acting or by telling long circumstantial tales, and histrionic exaggeration are part of everyday behavior. In Italy and Italian-American communities, life would seem colorless without these touches of the *commedia dell'-arte*." (J. Papajohn and J. Spiegel, *Transactions in Families*. San Francisco: Jossey-Bass, 1975.) As time proceeds, though, we can expect that Italian-Americans will have less of a reputation for histrionic behavior while people from other ethnic groups may develop a capacity for greater expressiveness.

Alan and Regina have been married three years and are the parents of a two-year-old boy. Alan grew up in a Jewish family. His father, a stockbroker, had wanted Alan to follow him into the profession and into the firm for which he had worked for many years. Alan had no aptitude for stocks and bonds, however, and didn't even care for money too much. He wanted to be an actor. While playing in a production of *The Taming of the Shrew*, he met Regina, who also had a small role. She was of Italian parentage. What Alan liked about her was not only her long hair and sparkling eyes but that "she was always acting, both offstage as well as on." He was captivated by the drama and excitement that she brought into his life. The drama was now getting to be too much, though. Their son was in the midst of the "terrible twos," and Alan did not relish coming home to the barrage of complaints from Regina about how aggravated she had become at the baby's behavior. "Why do you have to go out to rehearsals or interviews while I have to stay home with the 'sorcerer's apprentice'?" she said one day. They decided that professional counseling was in order. Alan came away convinced that Regina was still the same person with whom he had fallen in love four years before. She was born to act, a pattern of behavior inherited from her family. Just as he was able to set aside his theater role when the play was over, he resolved to treat Regina's exaggerated complaints about the baby's behavior in the same way. He would listen and give her some words of reassurance, but no more would he allow her complaints about the baby to "get to" him. The "terrible twos" would soon be over.

THE WAY
TO HAPPINESS

We have discussed some of the factors you should be conscious of in an interreligious marriage. Now we will outline some of the things we think you should do as you seek a happy married life together. The real work, of course, is up to you.

Be secure in your own identity. We are what we are—Jew, WASP, Italian, Black, Asian, Hispanic. This remains true even if we marry across ethnic or religious lines. Only when we accept what we ourselves are can we accept and appreciate others and the heritage they bring to a relationship. The great commandment in the Bible is to "love your neighbor as yourself." First we accept and love ourselves; then we are able to give love to others.

Share common interests and concerns. This is a basic requirement for any marriage. Opposites may attract for a while, but if there are not sufficient common interests and concerns, the attraction soon dissipates.

Be respectful of each other's background. This, too, is a basic requirement for any marriage. In an interreligious situation, though, there is the added respect that must be shown in word and in deed for a spouse's religious and ethnic heritage.

Seek to participate in each other's religious life. Keeping a respectful distance from your spouse's religious life is better than disparaging it, but sharing your dual religious heritage with each other and with your children is what you should strive for. Families need to share a past as well as a present and future. By understanding and sharing in religious celebrations, even if you don't necessarily subscribe to the theology behind them, you help to build a common family heritage.

Don't let others upset you. While you should always be kind and respectful to your own parents and your in-laws, this does not mean you should give in to them if they are unsympathetic to the kind of interreligious family life you seek to build. If you do not allow parents or in-laws to deter you from the path you wish to follow, then of course you should resist the efforts of other family members or well-meaning "friends" as well.

Contact sympathetic counselors. There are probably clergy (rabbis, priests, ministers) or other counselors in your community who are sympathetic to the problems of interreligious families whom you could contact when you need help. If you do not know of anyone close by, write to any of the authors of this book in care of Religious Books Editor, Macmillan Publishing Company, 866 Third Avenue, New York, New York 10022.

Recognize that you have much in common. Jews and Christians share a great deal of religious teaching, and you as a family share not only these common religious elements but many other aspects of life as well. There is much more that unites you than divides you.

Acknowledge that God wishes people to live in loving community. Though there were religious wars and persecutions in the past, we rejoice that now we seek to work together, building the kingdom of God on earth.

11

LIVING EXAMPLES: INTERRELIGIOUS FAMILIES IN THE UNITED STATES

Even though interreligious marriage is very common, there are still quite a number of people who will say that such unions are replete with insoluble problems. In the previous chapters we have endeavored to demonstrate that this does not have to be the case. We have outlined a framework for a family life in which both Judaism and Christianity can be represented in an atmosphere of acceptance and respect. We have presented what we hope is a sound theoretical basis for an intermarried family life, and we have brought forth a number of examples from the lives of real people to illustrate the points we wished to make.

Now, in addition, we will let families from all over the country speak for themselves. Some are people we have known for years. Others are people whom we have interviewed for the purpose of this book. All of them, however, whether from North, East, South, or West, have found a way to share a love for each other and for their children in a context that emphasizes the beauty and the inspiration that is inherent in both Judaism and Christianity. These are living examples of what life in an interreligious family can be. If you have chosen or will choose this type of life for yourself, we hope the examples presented here will give you a vision and goal toward which to strive.

Richard and Kathy

Richard and Kathy had hoped to be married in a joint Jewish-Catholic ceremony. Unable to make the arrangements for this, they were married instead in a Catholic ceremony. They have two children, both boys, who are receiving their religious education at the Reform temple in St. Paul, Minnesota. Richard is an attorney; Kathy has a background in nursing, but at present is quite busy with running her home and with volunteer activities in the community. Richard grew up as a Jew in Minneapolis, while Kathy comes from a Catholic family in Macon, Georgia.

The boys do not feel out of place in their temple's religious school because about one third of the children in their class are of mixed religious backgrounds. What is unique about them, however, is that Kathy, their Catholic mother, is in charge of all of the Sunday

School holiday celebrations that take place in their Jewish school. She feels fully accepted by the temple community and participates in all aspects of the children's religious life and education.

Richard and Kathy attend services at the temple about once a month as well as Catholic Mass on occasion. At home they observe the holidays of both faiths. According to a feature article in the local newspaper, dated December 25, 1982, Richard and Kathy's home "looks like any other house where young children live except it has more than its share of holiday decorations. From the street one can see a plump red-faced Santa Claus bellowing out a hearty 'Season's Greetings.' Next to Santa on the door is a poster of the traditional Jewish toy, a colorful dreidel or spinning top, with the words 'Happy Hanukkah' adding to the holiday hospitality." Kathy admits, though, that it's "sometimes a little difficult knowing my husband and sons don't share the same spiritual feelings at Christmastime. Last year we went home to Georgia for Christmas, and it was really fun for me. My nephew was in a Christmas pageant, and the whole family went to see it. It was a very moving pageant, especially for me. Then about halfway through, when Jesus had been born and everyone had gathered around the manger, my son leaned over and said, 'Mom, is it a boy or a girl?' From the beginning of our marriage, I agreed to raise the children Jewish. But they're going to know about my religion also. They're Jewish and I want them to know Judaism, but I also want them to understand Catholicism."

Richard and Kathy assert that religion is not a factor in their relationship with their in-laws, the children's grandparents. There is a mutual respect and love that binds the family together, including a respect for the various religious traditions that each side brings. They all enjoy various ethnic foods, and the family sings Jewish songs and Christmas carols. The only religious problem they have had to face is that they are the only Jews in the public school they attend.

Both Catholicism and Judaism, Richard and Kathy agree, teach the same moral code. During the years of their courtship and marriage they came to understand that the two religions are not that different in the essentials of life. Their common faith in God has enabled them to surmount the normal problems any couple has to face in a contemporary marriage. They have also received emotional support from their involvement in the "mixed doubles" group for interfaith couples sponsored by the temple.

Michael and Liv

How many Jewish men from New York travel on a tour to Norway, meet and marry one of the tour's guides, and then settle in Minnesota so that they can remain in touch with Norwegian culture? Michael did just that. He and his wife Liv and their infant son will preserve and celebrate the heritage of Norway in the pattern of their lives together. Their home is bilingual and, in addition to gefilte fish, matza ball soup, and knishes, the family table provides *lefse* (a Norwegian taco), Norwegian potato dumplings, and lamb with cabbage.

Mike is a social worker, while Liv occasionally cares for young children during the day, along with her own son. A Lutheran, on Sundays she is choir director at an Episcopal church. They attend Jewish services on Friday nights from time to time, but of course Liv is in church every Sunday because of her choir responsibilities. Every Christmas, though, she and her husband attend a Norwegian Lutheran church. Their son had a ritual circumcision and immersion in the ritual bath, ceremonies of conversion to Judaism.

The holidays of both Judaism and Christianity are celebrated with full panoply. On the Jewish High Holy Days they attend the temple. On Hanukkah they light the candles and exchange presents each night. On Christmas they decorate their tree with both angels and Hanukkah symbols. They send and receive Christmas gifts, attend a late-afternoon service in the Norwegian church, have a big dinner, and read the Nativity story in Norwegian. One of the appetizers at dinner is *lutefisk* (cod soaked in lye), a traditional Norwegian Christmas dish. They follow the Norwegian custom of singing carols while circling the Christmas tree. On the four Sundays preceding Christmas they light Advent candles, singing a song each week. The Passover Seder is also a major occasion at Mike and Liv's house. They always have a number of guests and plan to continue the tradition even if they should someday move to Norway, a possibility to which they have given much consideration.

Liv is an accomplished musician, and she brings Jewish as well as Norwegian music into their home. In fact, when she was conducting her church choir in Norway, she introduced some Hebrew songs into the repertoire long before she met her husband. Though a very devoted Lutheran Christian, she welcomes the

Jewish culture into her home because, as she says, "my religion is built on Judaism." Both Michael and Liv feel that marrying someone not of your own religion makes you examine your own spiritual nature and come to terms with what is really important to you. The spiritual feelings they share with each other, and with which their young son is being raised, are exemplified in the song they sing at mealtimes and at bedtime: "You who feed the birds, we thank You for feeding us too."

Robin and Pam

Robin and Pam run a computer consulting business together out of their new home in St. Paul, Minnesota. Robin, who is Jewish, grew up in Kentucky, while Pam, a Catholic of German extraction, is a native of Minnesota. They have three young daughters. What is unique about their family is that they have deliberately decided to raise their daughters with an equal involvement in Catholicism and Judaism. They do not send the girls for religious instruction to either church or temple, but they arrange readings, discussions, and holiday observances within the home.

Things were not always this way. A couple of years ago, three families set up their own "religious school," meeting weekly in homes. Now, however, other activities interfere, so this collective arrangement has ceased. Robin and Pam's children are disappointed that this has happened, but their parents will do their best to give them an understanding of the teachings of both religions. When people ask the girls about religion, they reply, "We are both Jewish and Catholic."

Robin and Pam attend High Holy Day services at the temple with their daughters as well as Christmas and Easter services at church. They attend Friday night services at the temple about six times a year, when there is a special program for children. If the Catholic church had something similar, they would attend those services too. They observe Hanukkah by lighting the candles each night and exchanging presents on one night. For Christmas they have a tree, a crèche, and an exchange of gifts. Christmas eve is always spent at Pam's parents' house. If Hanukkah should fall on Christmas eve, they bring their menorah with them and light the candles at the grandparents' house. Passover is celebrated with a Seder, and Robin eats matza instead of bread for the full week of the holiday. On Easter there is a family gathering and an egg hunt. On Friday nights the Sabbath candles are lit, and the wine and the bread are blessed. At weekday meals, too, there are nondenominational prayers of thanks. At bedtime the girls have been taught to recite the Angel of God, the Our Father, and the Shema in Hebrew and English. On Purim the family attends the carnival held at the temple, and on St. Nicholas Day, December 6, the children set out their shoes at night and find a present in the morning.

This is a household in which there is a pervasive emphasis on spirituality. Robin and Pam want their daughters to grow up recognizing the common spiritual elements in both Catholicism and Judaism. They don't want them to regard the temple as "daddy's place" and the church as "mommy's" but as *family* places where parents and children go for both inspiration and, on occasion, fun. Robin and Pam assert they have more religion in their home than most other families even though their children are not being sent to any formal religious training. Not all issues have been resolved, though. Pam would prefer that the children be baptized and have more involvement with Catholicism, and she and Robin continue to discuss this possibility. Robin would prefer a less ambiguous Jewish identity for the children. They both realize that compromise and mutual respect is what marriage is all about, and through open discussion of the issues and the possibilities they have been able to appreciate each other and where each is coming from. The girls, too, have benefited. Someday they may wish to go to the temple's Sunday School and have a Bat Mitzvah ceremony, and if they should wish to do this, it would be their own decision rather than one made for them by their parents. It would be an informed decision, too, for their parents are taking the responsibility of seeing that they learn the teachings and ideals of both religions, both through precept and example.

Robin and Pam say they encourage everyone to have an interreligious marriage because, in addition to the opportunities for learning and dialogue that it provides, it also eliminates the problem of deciding with which side of the family to spend Christmas and with which side to spend Passover.

Steven and Julie

Another interreligious couple living in St. Paul, Minnesota, is Steven and Julie. They have no children yet but look forward to having them. They feel that attempting to come to a decision about their children's religion in advance of pregnancy is unwise because it might have the effect, in their case as well as in other families, of postponing pregnancy until the issue is resolved. Children should be desired and loved irrespective of the religion in which they will be raised. For this reason, they say, they await the birth of a child without having decided upon its religion. Besides, prebirth agreements are often broken, opening up the possibility of marital discord and strife. When a child has actually arrived they will discuss the religious training they wish it to receive. Given the love and the mutual respect they share for each other, as well as for the child to come, they do not feel the decision they make will be anything but the right one for them and for their child.

Steve and Julie both grew up in Minnesota. He is Jewish and she is Catholic, of French and Italian descent. They were married in an ecumenical ceremony by a rabbi and a priest. Steve is a manager in a computer software company, while Julie is an accountant. They go to church about once a month and to the temple about four times a year. They also participate in the mixed doubles group at the temple.

When Julie told her parents about her plan to marry Steve, they were dismayed over the possibility that her children might not be Catholic. Her mother wept in sorrow over the destiny of these unborn children, while her father said that if Steve was really serious about marrying her, he should be willing to father Catholic children. Steve's parents were initially thrilled by his decision to marry since he was already "up in years" (twenty-eight). Soon thereafter they were struck by the seriousness of the situation and indicated they were not thrilled by the thought of Catholic grand-children. Steve and Julie have remained in close contact with their parents, but each describes the relationship with the respective in-laws as proper but "aloof." One of the things Julie objects to is that Steve's parents send her a Christmas card and Steve a Hanukkah card. She feels that any holiday card, whether Christmas or Hanukkah, should be addressed to both of them.

Steve and Julie celebrate the various holidays together. On Rosh Hashana and Yom Kippur they attend the temple. On Hanukkah they light the candles, Steve and Julie reciting the blessings alternately each night. On Christmas they exchange gifts, decorate a tree, and attend midnight Mass. At Passover they attend the Seder at Steve's parents' home. On Easter they attend church. Steve and Julie took a three-month course in Judaism together, as well as a similar course in Catholicism.

Steve and Julie agree that whatever problems they have, religious or otherwise, can be worked out. The key is open communication and mutual respect. They must make their own decisions, not their parents or their friends. The marriage they have, together with the love that infuses it, is worth whatever problems they might have now or in the future.

Stanley and Sandra

In New York City there are not only many interreligious marriages but also many interracial marriages. Stanley and Sandra exemplify both, since Stanley is black and Christian (African Methodist Episcopal) while Sandra is white and Jewish. He was born in North Carolina but grew up in Washington, D.C., and holds degrees from Harvard in both law and business. She is a New Yorker with a master's degree and works as an editor and freelance writer. They have no children as yet but look forward to them with eager anticipation.

Stanley's parents were not enthusiastic about his marriage to Sandra because they felt that in a sense he was deserting the black community. Sandra's parents were not that happy with their going together, but when they decided on marriage, they accepted it wholeheartedly. Now there is a warm and loving relationship with all of their parents, though Sandra feels Stanley's mother is still somewhat cool to her.

Stanley and Sandra attend High Holy Day services together, and when they visit his family in Washington, they sometimes go to church. On Hanukkah they light candles and exchange presents. On Christmas they set up a tree, exchange presents, and go to Washington to be with his family. On Passover they attend a Seder, either with friends or at the temple. On a more mundane level they enjoy both Jewish food and soul food.

Stanley has a very positive view of Judaism. Sandra had been rather ignorant of Christianity but is now very impressed with the role it has played as a source of guidance and inspiration to black Americans. She has taken a course that compares Judaism with Christianity so as to be better prepared when they have children. For Sandra the decision to get married was a major crisis in her life; she thought for a time that it might be the wrong thing to do. Now, however, they are united in the conviction that learning more about each other's heritage is a form of spiritual growth.

215

Their willingness to face uncertainty together, to decide their destiny as they share their lives and their love, is also a form of growth that they embrace and cherish.

Fred and Dawn

There have been several allusions to Fred and Dawn in earlier chapters in this book. Fred, who is an officer in his temple, says that "there is more religion in our family than if I had married a Jew." He feels that his marriage to Dawn, a Catholic of Italian parentage, has stimulated this involvement with his religion and inspired him to want to pass it on to his children, two rambunctious boys ages five and three.

Dawn attends her church two or three times a month. Their older son attends Immaculate Conception kindergarten in a suburb of New York City but during summers he goes to Temple Beth El's camp. The kindergarten's religious instruction emphasizes morality rather than doctrine: Hatred is something to be avoided, what God wants is love and compassion for others. At home, Dawn attempts to supplement the work of the school. Matthew says the Our Father at bedtime.

Fred and Dawn are people of high intelligence and good taste, and they agree that in some ways an interreligious marriage has unique problems that must be faced. They say that people have to really care for each other and perhaps work harder at their marriage than if they shared the same religion or were equally uninterested in religion. They take care to respect each other's feelings and avoid references that might be taken as ethnic slurs. Some think that an interreligious marriage is likely to fail, and Fred and Dawn want to prove them wrong.

If there are people who think that Fred and Dawn's marriage might not last, their parents are not among them. Their wedding ceremony was conducted by both a rabbi and a priest, and both sets of parents as well as other relatives and friends still recall the beautifully moving ceremony. When each of the boys was born, a priest and a rabbi came to their home to name and bless them in the presence of a large gathering from both sides of the family. Whenever the two sides of the family get together, which is often, there is always a great deal of warmth and camaraderie that crosses religious and ethnic lines.

Fred is an officer in a restaurant consulting firm; Dawn works as a physical therapist. They had originally decided they would raise their sons, if they had any, as Jewish and their daughters as Catholic. Now, however, they lean in the direction of giving all their children a Jewish identity. They have not decided if this will mean formal religious schooling and a Bar Mitzvah, but even if it does, Dawn will take the children to church fairly often so they can learn about Catholicism too. Fred and Dawn want their children to encounter religion as a learning experience, in addition to ethnic traditions and celebrations. The family goes together to High Holy Day services. On Hanukkah the candles are lit and the Hanukkah story told. Christmas is the time for gift-giving, a tree, and a trip to spend the day with Dawn's family. Passover finds the family at a Seder, either at home or at the temple, while Easter is spent with Dawn's family at an egg hunt and dinner they host each year.

Fred and Dawn are people of high accomplishment who radiate charm and hospitality. When they were first married they agreed that if either of them died within five years, he or she would be buried in the burial plot of his or her parents. That time now has passed; their love for each other has grown and deepened over the years and they have agreed that when death comes they will be buried together so that the companionship they shared in life can continue symbolically into eternity.

Daryl and Phyllis

Daryl and Phyllis have made their home in northern California, where Phyllis is a professor of mathematics. Daryl is a freelance editor and photographer, and a poet. Phyllis grew up in Rochester, New York, where her family was very involved in organizing a Reform temple, while Daryl was raised in Utah as a Latter-Day Saint (Mormon). More important than his religious background, however, is the fact that Daryl is Chinese. The home that he and Phyllis have established reflects the cultures of both China and the Western world. Daryl's parents had originally opposed his marriage, but when their first child was born fourteen years ago, they greeted her arrival with joy. Now they are happy that Daryl is teaching Chinese to both his children (the second is a boy, eleven).

Daryl and Phyllis's daughter celebrated her Bat Mitzvah last year. The rabbi who officiated had been the rabbi of the temple in which Phyllis grew up. Even though Daryl does not participate in the activities of the temple, he has insisted that both his children get their religious training and Hebrew instruction in the temple's Sunday School. Now their daughter conducts Friday night services at the temple from time to time. About one third of the children in the temple's school come from interreligious families.

In accordance with Chinese custom, Daryl and Phyllis's children each had a "red egg party" at the age of one month. Guests, both family and friends, were invited to a Chinese restaurant in San Francisco. As part of the festivities each guest was presented with an egg dyed red, the color for long life and good fortune. In return, the guests gave red envelopes containing money for the use of the child, who was thus welcomed into life.

Daryl and Phyllis participate enthusiastically in the celebration of many holidays. At Hanukkah the family lights candles for eight nights and exchanges gifts. Christmas sees the house decorated with a tree and ornaments, as well as an annual potluck supper for friends and neighbors, from which all go forth for Christmas caroling through the neighborhood. At Passover there is a home Seder for twenty or so people on the first night, followed by attendance at the temple Seder on the second night. Chinese New Year, celebrated during February, is also a major occasion. Daryl and Phyllis host a potluck Chinese banquet for eight or ten families. Another Chinese New Year custom is the presentation of red envelopes with money to the unmarried children of friends and relatives. Young children love to receive them, but older ones are sometimes inspired to get married so they can begin passing out these envelopes rather than continue to receive them.

Daryl and Phyllis are people of high culture whose home is filled with books and music. They appreciate and enjoy the traditions of both East and West, and have raised a family in which both love and accomplishment are valued. They have not found it difficult to meld the values and traditions of Judaism with both the Confucian ideals of China and the family emphasis of Mormonism. They have encountered no problems based on their religious difference because they have found that "morally and ethically we are the same."

Martin and Miriam

Martin's father was Italian-Catholic, his mother an English Protestant. He grew up in Massachusetts, where he went to the Catholic church regularly. At age twenty-one he went to New York to seek his fortune as an actor. He works now in the international department of a bank on Wall Street. Miriam grew up in Brooklyn, the daughter of Jewish parents who were very involved in socialist causes. She has retained a concern for the underprivileged, the form of idealism in which she was raised. She earned a degree magna cum laude in English and drama, and now works as a drama teacher and librarian at a private school in New York City.

Martin and Miriam have been married for twenty years. Their older son, who is now eighteen, studied Jewish history and theology along with elementary Hebrew in preparation for his Bar Mitzvah, which he celebrated five years ago. He is now taking time off from college to tour Australia and Southeast Asia. Their younger son will celebrate his Bar Mitzvah this year (1988). Martin and Miriam attend services at their temple on the major Jewish holidays. They occasionally go to services at various Christian or Unitarian churches. Though he has not been active in Catholicism for many years, Martin would like his sons to go through the confirmation ceremony. He realizes, though, that this would be possible only if they themselves elect to become Christians and go through the instruction and rituals that lead to confirmation. Since his sons have chosen a Jewish identity, Martin acquiesces happily and participates fully at both temple services and holiday observances at home. He looks upon Judaism as "a beautiful religion."

Martin and Miriam observe the High Holy Days at the temple. At Hanukkah they light candles for the eight nights and have a dinner during the holiday with Miriam's parents, at which time gifts are exchanged. For Christmas they have a tree at home and occasionally an Advent calendar, a ritual encouraged by the private school to which the children have gone. At home they sometimes have carol-singing as well as the preparation of special foods and candies for distribution at the school's Christmas celebration. There is always a trip to Massachusetts for the holiday itself to be with Martin's extended family. The observance there includes a turkey dinner, attendance at a Unitarian church, and the intensive and serious exchange of gifts with just about everyone who makes an appearance. Passover is celebrated with a Seder at Miriam's parents' home. The family eats only matza for the week of the holiday (though Martin admits he does eat bread outside the house). From time to time they attend a church service on Easter.

Martin and Miriam are pleased with the school to which the boys have gone. It follows the philosophy of Rudolph Steiner and the Anthroposophical Society, promoting a kind of humanistic Christianity. Grace at meals is recited, and the school stresses the primacy of spiritual experience. Martin and Miriam feel this sense of awe and commitment to spiritual values is important as part of the educational process. Miriam has an interest in some forms of mystical Christianity, such as the work of Thomas Merton, but she still has to deal with subconscious feelings of resentment toward Christianity because of the Holocaust and some unpleasant experiences she had while growing up because she was a Jew. She has an even greater problem, however, with the materialistic aspects of the Christmas season. She finds the overwhelming commercialism of the season quite distasteful and sometimes ponders the possibility of joining some sort of evangelical group whose purpose would be to "put Christ back into Christmas."

Martin and Miriam agree that they hold similar spiritual values. Every marriage, they say, involves accommodation to different ways of thinking and different backgrounds. They maintain that it is false to assume one religion in a family is easier to deal with than two. Men and women usually think differently from each other, and this provides greater opportunities for conflict than religious differences. When two religions come together, the family has an opportunity for learning and spiritual enrichment.

Larry and Jane

Jane and Larry had been married for five years at the time of their interview. Because both were carefully nurtured in the traditions of their separate faiths by committed parents, and each is committed to and well educated in his and her own heritage, their marriage posed larger challenges than a marriage in which particular religious traditions are not so vital in the lives of the family. Though their experiences may sometimes appear unique, they serve as examples of how even the most difficult relationship can often be reconciled in the midst of a healthy marriage.

Larry and Jane met while in graduate school. They had both dated extensively, and when they began spending time with each other, they were aware that marriage was a distinct possibility in their lives. Jane, a Protestant Christian, already had a graduate degree in religious studies and had grown up in as mature and involved a liberal Christian family as one could imagine. Larry was similarly nurtured in a close and committed Orthodox Jewish family, where no one in memory had married outside the Jewish tradition. He, too, was vitally interested in religion and cherished his Jewish heritage.

Now in their late twenties, Jane and Larry knew what they were looking for in a spouse. Though both had dated individuals from different religious traditions, they had not given serious thought to marrying a person of a different faith. Soon, however, their relationship became more than a sharing of mutual interests and activities. Both Larry's and Jane's parents knew they were dating, but since their university was not in either's home town, the situation did not, at first, create great difficulties.

However, when Jane wrote her parents that she was moving in with Larry, a potential crisis began to build. Her mother found two reasons to object. First, she felt that Larry's strong Jewish commitment surely meant that he had no intention of marrying her daughter and was simply taking advantage of Jane's affection. Second, if they were to marry later, didn't her daughter know that a marriage between an Orthodox Jew and a committed Protestant Christian was fraught with disaster? Larry's family lived farther away, so for a while the question of his relationship with Jane was barely raised. However, he knew from his father's past comments that marriage to a non-Jew was anathema to him.

Time only brought Jane and Larry closer together. Within months discussion turned to marriage. They visited each other's family home, and the atmosphere, while cordial, was strained. Jane knew of her family's tension about their plans but was not prepared when her mother, ordinarily a very open, accepting person, unhesitatingly proclaimed that the cultural and religious differences between them could never be bridged. Her father took Jane for a walk in the park and asked her to give serious thought about how confusing and unfair such a marriage would be for their children. He advised his daughter that they would not be able to live in the mid-sized city where they now attended school, but would have to move to a larger urban center so that they and their children would not experience rejection. Larry was summoned home to his parents and asked to sign papers giving up all claim on his family or to any inheritance if he married outside his own tradition. So convinced was Larry's father that Jane was not committed to his son, that Jane recalls his asking her, "What would it take for you not to marry my son?" Both faced major rejection from their families for the first time in their lives.

Larry and Jane, in a series of conversations and also with counseling from others, decided that their strength lay in not wavering from their commitment to each other. Ready to risk the worst, they felt that their best hope for reconciliation with their families was to affirm their plans without hesitation. Jane recalled that one of the individuals who counseled her suggested that she "walk through life like the heroine of a novel."

Both sets of parents also sought help—Larry's with their rabbi, Jane's with their minister. In each case, the parents were counseled that their objections were probably not going to be successful and that tensions between religious traditions should not be the basis of severing precious family ties. Jane's parents sadly and reluctantly accepted the inevitable, but energetically set out to plan with their daughter for her upcoming marriage. Larry's mother, never as determined as her husband that her son marry only a Jew, sought a reconciling position. But with less than two weeks before the wedding, Larry's father remained firm in his declaration that he would not attend the wedding or have anything further to do with his son. Finally, a letter written to Larry's father from his brother reminded him that their own Orthodox Jewish father would have never taken such an adamant position. This, plus a continuing flow of positive advice and counsel from other friends and family members, resulted in the father's reconsideration of his position and decision to join in the wedding celebration. Many forces were working together to bring reconciliation. Larry and Jane pursued every one they could.

Jane and Larry continued to search for ways to bridge the chasm between their families. A week prior to the wedding the groom's parents traveled to his bride's hometown and met her family. Larry and Jane hosted a dinner party where the two sets of parents were deliberately seated together at a table limited to four. While the parents confessed that they "stayed away from controversial subjects," they grew better acquainted and discovered that they did enjoy one another's company. Larry and Jane finally remember how, as the wedding day grew closer, each family competed to see which could do more to add to the marriage festivities. To affirm the heritage of both partners, the wedding took place not in the bride's church, as is traditional among Christians, but in her parents' garden. Her family's pastor gladly officiated and was joined by a congenial rabbi who traveled from another city because none of the local rabbinate would officiate at an interfaith marriage.

Through all of these preparations, Jane and Larry continued to discuss the basis of their marriage. For Jane, who cherished her Christian heritage, conversion was not an option. Larry shared an identical commitment to his Orthodox Jewish tradition. Before the wedding, however, they decided that any children they had would be raised as Jews, but that Jane would also celebrate her religious faith both in her church and at home with the family. The children would be given a broad understanding of the traditions of their mother's faith. They have continued to live in a mid-sized Southern American city and have found a small group of friends with whom they can discuss their interfaith relationships. They observed that, among both Jews and Christians, the institutional settings of their faiths accept persons of interfaith marriage but do not easily assimilate them. However, they find friends among both Jews and Christians through the varied interests they share.

Jane and Larry commented that few of their peers could understand anything of the difficulty their marriage posed. Most of their friends could be considered religious persons, but not as deeply committed to their own traditions as were either Jane or Larry or their parents. On the other hand, Jane and Larry concluded that their marriage was enhanced by the challenges which they had successfully faced.

Neither set of parents has completely accepted the marriage, although both are discovering in their new son- and daughter-in-law an individual they respect and admire. Relationships are no longer strained, and because of the geographic distance between the in-laws, many of the difficulties faced by families living in the same community are avoided. Larry is now reconciled with his father and has been fully accepted back within the family.

The most recent event in their lives has been the birth of their first child, Joseph. Both families came together after the birth to help their children, but some of the old "tapes" were replayed. Jane's parents excused themselves from Joseph's circumcision, not in opposition to the tradition, but because the ceremony was too exotic for their approach to faith. However, both sets of grandparents celebrate having a grand-child. Jane and Larry emphasized that though many friends had advised them that a baby would "bring round" both their families to a closer relationship, Joseph's birth was not the catalyst. Long before the child was born, carefully planned encounters of the families and their own discussions about their marriage had already made possible the process of reconciliation. Larry and Jane felt it was a dangerous course to assume that a new baby would "mend the fences." They pointed out that having a baby sometimes causes more tension as each family competes regarding the child's religious development.

The decision to raise Joseph as a Jew proved even more challenging than Larry had anticipated. Because a child's Jewish heritage is established through the mother, the only alternative open to them to give their son a Jewish legacy was by the child's own conversion.

After many inquiries, a rabbinical court was convened in another state some distance from their home. Jane was interrogated in depth about her knowledge and understanding of Jewish tradition and law, and about the nature of her Christian commitment. It was of utmost importance for the court to ascertain that her understanding of Christianity did not negate Judaism as a valid faith superseded by Christianity. She was able to affirm this without hesitation, asserting that for her the Christian faith does not at all negate the covenant of God with the Jews. She views Christianity as an enhancing of the covenantal relationship, as have many divine-human encounters through the centuries. This process was successfully completed and their son, Joseph, will be raised fully as a Jew and recognized as such by the Jewish community. Again, it was their perseverance and informed background that made it possible for them to move through great challenge and difficulty.

In the home, Larry and Jane celebrate both Jewish and Christian customs and holidays. In their prayers and their festivities, they and both their families carefully plan activities so as not to inject words and traditions that appear to reject the other's heritage. Larry attends special services of worship with Jane, especially at Christmas. Her interest in church is centered around the choir and the Christmas music, which they agree is beautiful to both of them. Jane often goes with Larry to the Jewish discussion groups in which he participates and often finds herself in the position of a reconciler in areas where stereotypes exist about the two faiths.

They both share an awareness that many questions will be raised in the years ahead. Their child will surely ask questions about why his mother wanted him to be Jewish but was not willing to convert herself. Some Orthodox Jews will probably look upon Joseph's conversion with misgivings. However, Jane and Larry are convincing when they conclude that they can give each other and their children a supportive, meaningful heritage and grow together in their family life.

Many interfaith couples probably will not face the same challenges as they, nor will they feel the need to retain some of the more firmly established traditions of each faith. To continue an Orthodox Jewish tradition within an interfaith marriage is probably the most challenging approach of all. However, their experience is a loving example that informed commitment by both members of an interfaith marriage to their own traditions and an empathetic understanding of the faith of each spouse can be the means by which an interfaith marriage can flourish, a child can be given a strong heritage, and neither partner will necessarily lose essential dimensions of his or her own experience and practice of religious faith.

Irwin and Betty

Betty and Irwin met in New York City during the 1950s. Irwin grew up in a Conservative Jewish family and had only known and dated Jewish girls until he graduated from college and entered law school. During that period he began to enjoy the company of friends from a variety of backgrounds, who were welcome in his home. However, when he told his parents he was going to marry Betty, a Protestant Christian who had been nurtured in the Church since childhood, he found considerable opposition, especially from his father. He had anticipated this and had delayed his decision to marry for some months because of it.

Betty is from a midwestern small town and had come to New York after finishing school. When she returned some years later with Irwin and announced their upcoming marriage, she was gratified that her mother and father were very supportive, and she assertively announced their approval in order to mute any criticism that might have been voiced among the family or in the community. Betty pointed out that Irwin was much more mature and friendly than many of the other young men that she had known. Her family was relieved, impressed, and grateful for her "good sense" in finding such a delightful son-in-law, Jewish or not, and they didn't raise the usual question about whether the children would be raised in the Christian or Jewish tradition.

As the wedding date drew near, Irwin's father sought means to delay it, thinking that the relationship would perhaps erode if he could only postpone the event. He talked privately with both Irwin and Betty, but to no avail. Irwin had learned early on in the relationship that Betty would not convert to Judaism and counseled his father against raising that question with her. Since this was the first time anyone in the family had married outside Judaism, and Irwin was the oldest son, his father knew instinctively that this would open the door to other interfaith marriages. Irwin also felt that factors other than "faith" were at work. Neither he nor his brothers had previously challenged their father's will to such a degree. Irwin knew that for his father the prospect of an interfaith marriage meant a breakdown in their family of the historic identity of their Jewish culture and heritage. Though Irwin admits that he cherishes his Jewish identity, he firmly believes that a personal relationship with someone you love and respect is far more important than religious differences.

Irwin's parents refused to attend the wedding, which was performed by a Justice of the Peace in a friend's home, partly in order not to offend Irwin's family. Because Irwin's parents would not attend, neither did Betty's. Their reasoning was that this would further alienate Irwin's parents. For a number of years Irwin and his father were not close, but Irwin and his mother, who was not nearly as adamantly opposed as his father, kept in regular contact.

Betty and Irwin had their first child five years after they were married. Early in their relationship they had decided together that their children would be raised in the Protestant Christian tradition. Irwin believed that since the mother would have the major role in nurturing their children, their religious identification should be left primarily in her hands. Betty recalled that she would have felt very inadequate nurturing their children in Jewish traditions. Their three boys grew up attending Sunday School, were baptized and confirmed in a mainline Protestant denomination, and have continued to identify themselves as Christian. Each is also proud of his Jewish heritage. They are all now university students.

The birth of their first child helped considerably with the reconciliation of Irwin's father with his son and family. In spite of the father's opposition to his son's interfaith marriage, Irwin and Betty's marriage proved to be the most stable among his children. Betty's openness to and support of her husband's family were major factors in improving relationships. She encouraged their sons to go with their father and grandfather to synagogue services and participated with the family in High Holy Day celebrations in the home. As a result, a close bonding between the paternal grandparents and the children developed. This was especially cherished in their grandfather's later years as a widower. Irwin, also, often participated with his father in the synagogue, and together they renewed their identification with their Jewish heritage.

At Christmas and Easter, Irwin often would accompany his family to church, if not only for worship, but also for the other activities surrounding the season. Betty recalled that after years of avoiding their home when the Christian tree was in place, Irwin's father finally relented and in later years joined them for Christmas dinner. Both husband and wife emphasized their commitment to support the other's traditions and expressions of faith.

One interesting observation was made: Irwin's father showed off his grandsons to his friends in the synagogue but never revealed that they were not being raised as Jews. The sons today affirm that they are very much at home in Jewish as well as Christian settings and have no hesitation participating in their father's traditions. The parents conclude that much of this attitude stems from the relaxed, although not casual, approach both father and mother had toward religion. The ethical and spiritual dimensions of life are precious to them, but neither felt nor communicated any hint that one faith was superior to or had greater validity than the other. They celebrated common ground whenever they could. Irwin confessed that he has on occasion secretly nourished the hope that his sons might one day choose to identify with their father's religious heritage. His reasoning is much like his father's: Irwin's need for the identification of his proud heritage to continue in the family. Betty understands this need and would not stand in the way if this were to be the decision of any of their sons.

A further interview with one of Betty and Irwin's sons revealed his grateful affirmation of his parents' ability to be honest and open with him and his brothers by reinforcing each other's traditions and sharing each of their heritages without mandating that their sons accept them uncritically or exclusively. He appreciated the strong ethical, liberating attitudes of his parents, who themselves had refused to join either Jewish or Christian groups that discriminated against persons on the basis of religion or race. He underscored that the children were given a respect for and pride in both their religious traditions, and felt that they had a certain advantage over children nurtured exclusively in one tradition. He stated that his own Christian faith was an inclusive and open commitment, adding that it was at least as strong and informed as the majority of his peers whose backgrounds were not of an interfaith nature.

12

CAN TWO RELIGIONS COEXIST *HAPPILY* IN ONE HOME?

If you have read the preceding chapters, you know that our answer to the question, Can two religions coexist in one home?, is definitely *yes*. We have presented examples of families in different parts of the country, and we have drawn upon our own experiences and insights as clergy—Jewish, Catholic, and Protestant. It can be asserted without any doubt that it is possible for two religions to coexist in one home.

The more important question, however, is: Can two religions coexist *happily* in one home? Various pamphlets and broadsides about Jewish-Christian intermarriage attempt to convey the idea that this is impossible to achieve. Jews, these articles maintain, grow up with a subliminal distaste for the symbols, rituals, and theology of Christianity, and whether they realize it or not, they cannot possibly be happy in a home where Christianity is present. Christians, on the other hand, are deprived of true happiness and satisfaction if they are prevented from bringing elements of Christianity into the home. These texts go on to teach, therefore, that Jews should marry Jews, and Christians should marry Christians. If this is not possible, then the Christian should convert to Judaism. As for Jews who insist that they have no problem with relating to Christian symbols and practices, these texts assert that such people are not *really* Jews. They are, by definition, materialistic or self-centered, or devoid of any understanding of the heritage of their people. If such people are no longer included within the ranks of Judaism, then the assertions made by these texts become self-fulfilling prophecies, and it follows that no *real* Jew could possibly be happy in a home where Christianity is present.

Our attitude is quite the opposite, of course. We do not expel from Judaism all those whose attitudes do not happen to coincide with the prejudices of the polemicists against intermarriage. In our work we see an ever-expanding band of Jewish men and women, now in the hundreds of thousands but eventually to be in the millions, who have married or plan to marry Christians. We have found that families of this type have the potential to find happiness and satisfaction and that their children can grow up as well adjusted as any others. Yes, by all means two religions can coexist happily in one home. But, as in any marriage, you have to work at it for this consummation to occur.

This book has been our attempt to show you some of the things that you can do as you work within the context of an interreligious marriage. As in any family, your life together must be based on mutual respect, out of which love develops and grows. You also need an active desire to learn about and participate in each other's heritage of faith. You must share both Judaism and Christianity with your children, though ideally they should grow up identifying one faith or the other as their own. A child in an interreligious family should be able to say, "I am a Jew (or a Christian); my mother is a Jew (or a Christian), and my father is a Christian (or a Jew)." Neither faith should be presented as "better" than the other. Your children need to know that they share in both of them and that they are not strangers in either context. As your children grow in the love of God and their fellow men and women, you will be able to observe their development and rejoice that you, their parents, discovered each other and founded a family.

Given the tremendous number of interreligious families that will come into being during the years to come, what will be the effect on Judaism and Christianity as organized religious systems? We are not prophets, but we are willing to hazard a guess or two as to what may occur. Christianity will continue to emphasize its Jewish roots, a process that began before interreligious marriage had reached such a tremendous volume. Judaism will, as time goes on, come to look upon Christianity not as a rival but as its partner in the redemption of God's world. Neither faith will characterize the other as "false" or "inadequate," nor will "conversion" from one faith to the other be advocated. We do not envision, nor do we advocate, a "syncretism," a combination of the two religions, but we see a time when a loving acceptance of Jews by Christians, and of Christians by Jews, will take place, for both communities constitute "God's people." This process, though it might occur without intermarriage, will be hastened by the large number of interreligious families. If a husband, wife, and children can live together in mutual respect and love, so, too, can the religious communities. This is a lesson that interreligious marriage will be able to teach.

Genesis teaches, "God created man in His own image, in the image of God He created him; male and female He created them. And God blessed them and said to them, 'Be fruitful and multiply and fill the earth.' . . . God saw everything that He had made and behold, it was very good." This is the image that faith presents to us, both Jews and Christians. This is the image that it is our destiny to fulfill.

INDEX

Index

Religion *(continued)*
  See also Christianity; Conver-
    sion: Judaism; Interreligious
    marriage
Religious holidays, 109–31
  dual heritage, involvement of
    family in, 130
  family traditions and, 110
  "misgivings" about others'
    holiday, 110
  Sabbaths and, 110–13
  See also individual holidays
Resurrection, 40, 44, 67–68
Rosary Prayer, 47
Rosh Hashana, 26–27, 114–15

Sabbath, 25–26, 45–46, 110–13,
    183
  in Christianity, 45–46, 113–14
  in Judaism, 25–26, 111–12
Saturnalia, Roman feast of, 119
Second Vatican Council (1965),
    50
Seder, 29, 45, 124–26
  Passover, 124–26
Sephardic Jews, 161
Shabuot, 29
Shiva, 167
Solemnity of Mary, Mother of
    God, 57
Southern Baptist churches, 64
Spiegel, J., 201
Suggestions for successful
    interreligious marriage,
    202–04

Sukka, 27, 116
Sukkot, 27
Sunday School, 114, 178
Synagogues, 20–21

Talmud, 19
Ten Commandments, 16, 26,
    29, 54
Torah, 17, 25
Transactions in Families (Papajohn
    and Spiegel), 201
Trinity, 54

*Uncommon Therapy: The Psychiat-
    ric Techniques of Milton H.
    Erickson* (Haley), 146
United Church of Canada, 61
United Church of Christ, 61
United Methodist Church, 61,
    62

Weddings. *See* Ecumenical
    wedding ceremony; Cath-
    olic weddings; Jewish
    wedding ceremony; Prot-
    estant marriage rites
Wesley, Charles, 62
Wesley, John, 62

Yahweh, 16, 24, 157
Yarmulke, 22, 34
Yom Kippur, 26–27, 115

Zionism, 35